D0228937

THE TOWN PARSON

THE TOWN PARSON

HIS LIFE AND WORK

Being the substance of the Pastoral Theology Lectures delivered before the University of Cambridge, and at King's College, London, in the year 1914

NOW WRITTEN OUT AND ENLARGED
BY THE
REV. PETER GREEN, M.A.
RECTOR OF ST. PHILIP'S, SALFORD
CANON OF MANCHESTER
CHAPLAIN TO H.M. THE KING

WITH A PREFACE BY THE
RIGHT REV. EDWARD STUART TALBOT, D.D.
FORMERLY LORD BISHOP OF WINCHESTER

LONGMANS, GREEN AND CO.
LONDON ♦ NEW YORK ♦ TORONTO
1933

LONGMANS, GREEN AND CO. LTD.
39 PATERNOSTER ROW, LONDON, E.C.4
6 OLD COURT HOUSE STREET, CALCUTTA
53 NICOL ROAD, BOMBAY
36A MOUNT ROAD, MADRAS

LONGMANS, GREEN AND CO.
55 FIFTH AVENUE, NEW YORK
221 EAST 20TH STREET, CHICAGO
88 TREMONT STREET, BOSTON

LONGMANS, GREEN AND CO.
128–132 UNIVERSITY AVENUE, TORONTO

First published 1920
New Edition 1923 : New Impression 1932
Reissue in the Church Porch Library
August 1933

To all those who
having served their King and Country
in the Great War
desire now to serve the King of Kings
in the Ministry of His Church
and to the
Memory of the Fallen

I dedicate this Book
with Love and Gratitude

PREFACE

I UNDERTOOK to commend this book because the author wished it, and because after a friendship of a quarter of a century there is hardly anyone within my knowledge more fit to write what may really help the many who need help of the kind.

I can scarcely overestimate the value of such a book to beginners preparing for Ordination, and perhaps even more to those who, having been a year or more in Holy Orders, and knowing a little of the difficulties by experience, crave guidance and encouragement. They will note that what they find here is the work of one who is not only an expert craftsman intent upon the most sacred of crafts, but has also kept himself alert to observe, and remember, and appropriate, what is wise and suggestive in a wide area of reading and human experience. They will be struck by the combination of intensity and range; and will perhaps find that rich as the book is in practical teaching, the author's best gift to them is the unconscious influence of this living example.

I do most earnestly hope that in days when the lives of our younger clergy must be so hard beset by the alternative or combined dangers of hurried desultoriness and of professional narrowness, this little book, carrying so much within its covers, may go far and help much.

God bless its writer and his work!

EDW. WINTON.

Farnham Castle, Surrey.
November 13, 1919.

AUTHOR'S PREFACE TO NEW EDITION

The issue of a new edition of this book, while it affords no opportunity of altering the text, allows of the addition of a new Preface. And I am glad of the chance, for there are several things I want to say. No one, I should imagine, ever reads a book that he has written when it is actually in print without seeing many things he would like to alter. And as years pass the desire to add, to omit, to re-write, to express differently, grows stronger and stronger. So I hope no one will suppose that I am satisfied with this book. No one is more conscious of its faults than I am. But I am sure of one thing. However faulty the design of the book, and the execution of that design, it has one claim to notice. It treats a subject of supreme importance. I am convinced, and I grow daily more and more convinced, that next to the influence of the home—and by that I mean, the life and character of the parents, and especially of the mother—there is nothing so vital to the religious life of a nation as pastoral work. By it the Church as a whole daily lives and grows. A country which is supplied with the best possible Government Departments, with Ministers of Health, and of Commerce, and of Education, with Royal and Parliamentary Commissions on this, that, and the other, and with every description of controller, inspector, and adviser, but in which few or none cultivate the fields or work in the mines, is a country which is going to ruin. For it is true that 'the King himself is served by the field' (Eccles. v. 9). Equally a Church may have every description of organisation, movements, national, general, and parochial missions, conferences, summer schools, and what not, but if plain parochial work is neglected the Church will die from the roots upward.

And I fear I must express my own belief—in which of course, I may be, and earnestly trust that I am, quite wrong—that straight-forward, simple, day-in-day-out pastoral work in the parishes is not done to-day as it was a generation ago, and not done as it ought to be.

There are, of course, reasons for this, and even excuses. How can ordinary parish work fail to be neglected when parishes are undermanned to the extent that most are to-day? The population of England had increased out of all proportion to the increase in the number of the clergy, long before the war, and since the war the discrepancy is even more glaring. Nor are we even making the best use of the man-power we have. No thoughtful person can doubt that, apart from London as the seat of Parliament, and of the Executive of Government, the England that matters most is the great industrial districts of the Midlands and the North. But it is just in these dioceses, in Yorkshire,

Lancashire, and Durham, in the Potteries, and the parts about Birmingham, that the proportion of clergy to population is lowest. Yet an undermanned parish is not one merely where necessary work is left undone. It is one in which much that is done yields no returns because it cannot be followed up. Young people are lost to the Church because they cannot be looked after and shepherded in the critical years that follow their Confirmation; new comers to the parish drop into the category of confirmed non-churchgoers because they are not visited and welcomed; regular churchgoers are estranged because no one visits them when they are ill. And while this is going on the clergyman is taxing his strength to provide the legal minimum of services, to baptise, marry, and bury, and to visit such sick as he may hear of by chance, or as may send for him. If at any time he gets a free day there is little incentive to any special effort, since he feels that such an occasion will not occur again till all chance of garnering fruit from his previous effort has passed away. Anything like real pastoral work, still more anything in the nature of aggressive mission work, is out of the question. Yet it must be remembered that the ordinary congregation is maintained at its full strength by just these methods which are becoming daily more and more things of the past—by steady pastoral work in the homes, that is to say, and by careful shepherding of adolescents from the time they leave school till they settle down as regular members of the Church. With all the perfection of our organisation at the top, there is grave danger of the Church dying from the roots upward.

Indeed, I am not sure that the perfection of our organisation is not in itself one of the causes of our failure. Dr. Knox, a very keen sighted critic said, while he was still Bishop of Manchester, that the half century since his ordination had been marked by an immense development of the machinery of the Church, but that he often doubted whether there had been anything like a corresponding advance in spiritual life and power. My own experience extends over a much shorter period. Yet I feel that his doubt is well founded. May we not ask, indeed, whether in place of an advance comparable to our advance in organisation, there had not been an actual and positive decline ? All this machinery needs men to work it, and many a hard-working clergyman, who could give at the end of the week a good account for every hour of every day, has been so absorbed in ruri-decanal, diocesan, and general church business that his own parishioners hardly know him by sight. But the business man, clerk, or artizan in the parish is not brought to church, still less to an active participation in church work (and that is what the Church lives by and needs) by reading in the evening paper of the meeting, of the diocesan societies, or the opening of the National Assembly, but by the personal ministrations of his vicar.

But may we not, without injustice, go farther still and ask whether our spiritual leaders really value homely, day-in-day-out parish work ? Everything seems to be considered of importance except that by which the Church lives—namely steady pastoral work. If a young man shows exceptional ability and earnestness in his parish work everyone seems anxious to get him away to do something else. I hear one day that the new curate at St. Ichabod's is doing wonders with his lads, and making a great success of his Wednesday afternoon service for mothers. A few days after he bounds into my study to tell me that he has been appointed 'Commissioner for the North-west district of England' to 'organise the home base' for service abroad, or asked to be travelling secretary for the 'Society for Summer School for the application of psycho-analysis to Confirmation classes.' This noted vicar is granted a year's leave of absence from his parish for this purpose; and the other noted rector a year's absence from his parish for some other purpose. A little lip-service is paid from time to time to the value of parish work. But in this, as in so many things, our acts seem to give the lie to our words.

What is the cure? For to lament a state of things, yet offer no suggestions for improving it, is of little use. First and foremost, of course, church people at large, and not the bishops only, or indeed mainly, but the laity, must face the problem of an adequate supply of clergy. An undermanned church so far from being a church economically manned is a church wastefully and extravagantly manned. Often when the vicar of some great industrial parish tells me that his church cannot face the cost of an assistant priest I feel inclined to say, 'I am sure that is true. But if you would have faith, appoint not one curate but three, and work the parish as it ought to be worked, at the same time starting some form of Free-Will Offering Scheme; you would soon have more money than you need.' For the question of the proper payment of the clergy will be solved, if it is ever solved, not by the bishops but by the laity, and not by the diocese but by the parish.

Secondly, I am sure the clergy—and more especially the energetic, capable, hard-working, and zealous clergy—must exercise real self-denial and leave a great many things they now do themselves, to be done by the laity. They should 'give themselves continually to prayer, and to the ministry of the Word.' Many clergy complain that the laity won't take up the burden; or can't be relied on. I believe it is, in most cases, far more true to say that the clergy won't let them, and won't trust things out of their own hands. We parsons are too often a bossy, fussy, dictatorial lot.

But chiefly relief from the present distress must be sought along the lines of a new vision, on the part of the younger generation, of the worth, the dignity, and the happiness of pastoral work. And here I can speak with no uncertain voice. As I believe there is no work so needful, for the highest welfare of the Church and nation, as devoted pastoral work in the parishes, so I believe there is no life so full, so rich, so happy as that of the parish priest who really strives to know and to serve his people. If any young man will set before him the high ideal of being a true pastor, known and loved by all those whose souls are committed to his care, and will seek the help of God to realise that ideal to the utmost, he is certain very soon to feel the charm of the work, and to know that he has chosen his path in life wisely and well.

CONTENTS

CHAPTER VI

THE MANAGEMENT OF A PARISH

comes to know the parish, and the nature of his work, more intimately. But that is no reason for postponing so important a matter. For there are many things in a parson's life which make the careful and disciplined ordering of his time specially necessary. Among many such things we may notice three main ones. They are these: (i) Because a clergyman is so largely his own master from the very first. A young professional man, a lawyer or doctor or bank clerk or man in a business house, has a senior partner, or a man of some kind over him. He has also regular business hours, times when he must be at his desk or in his surgery or office. With a clergyman, even with a young curate working under the most careful and energetic of vicars, this is very much less so. It is true that a clergyman's hours may be, and often are, much longer, and the claims on his time and energies much more exacting, than is the case with any other professional man, with the possible exception of the doctor. But it is equally true that the clergyman is less tied to fixed hours of work, and in more danger of slipping, almost unconsciously, into slack and careless habits than other men of his class. A working man who for forty years had been indefatigable in church work, and had been brought into close contact with many clergymen, once said to me, 'It seems to me that a clergyman's work is very much what he likes to make it. If he has his heart in it he can work from morning to night, but if he likes he can make it a soft job. He is his own master.' Quite so; but, if you are to be your own master, take care that you are master of yourself.

And no man will ever master himself without rules; as the Psalms teach us, 'Wherewithal shall a young man cleanse his way? Even by ruling himself after Thy word.' And obviously the ruling and ordering of one's time must be a preliminary to all other forms of discipline.

(ii) A second reason which makes a time-table necessary is the fact that a clergyman has so many and such trifling details to attend to. No man has so many, and such various, duties to perform, and so many different places in which to perform them. The business man has probably a more or less detailed and systematised round of duties to perform. Indeed, one of the commonest complaints which we hear to-day is that work, in big business firms, tends to become so specialised that a man is all day long doing one and the same job. And even if the business man's work is varied and interesting, he has at any rate a single place, his office, in which to do it, and all sorts of helps to its orderly performance. Not so the clergyman. His day, unless he is very careful, will become a constant succession of trifles, and the church, the day schools, the parish, his own study, and a score of other places will all be claiming his attention at once. Business men often complain of the unbusinesslike habits of the clergy. I often wonder if many of them would do any better, or even as well, if they had to deal with the same bewildering mass of unconnected details, and to do so with no help from clerks, and office furniture and apparatus, and the orderly system of business method. But the question for us is not 'Do we do as well as our critics would under the same circumstances?' but, 'Do we do as well as possible?' And I am sure that if we want to be free from the horrid feeling that the day has passed in a whirl of distracting detail and that little or nothing has been accomplished, we must endeavour to order our time.

(iii) The third reason for having a time-table is the most important of all, and the one we are most likely to overlook. The claims on the time of a clergyman in a big town parish to-day are so overwhelming that no man can possibly do all there is to be done. Something must almost inevitably be neglected. But this being so, there is very real danger lest a man should day after day do those things which he likes and is interested in, and neglect those which are uncongenial to him. Some time ago a clergyman friend of mine was very indignant because some of his people suggested—or he thought that they suggested—that he was lazy and neglected his work. 'I am sure,' he declared, 'I work from morning to night. I never have a moment to myself.' Which I know was perfectly true. On the other hand, I strongly suspect that he spends a disproportionate amount of time on the things he is keen on, and entirely neglects the things that bore him. Now no man is equally interested in all parts of his work, or does all equally well, and so, if we just work on impulse, and without plain rules, we are very likely to neglect the less pleasant part of our work. But if a man draws up a time-table he is not likely to omit, in cold blood, the things he dislikes. On the other hand, if they find a place on his time-table and then, day by day, he finds that he has allowed other things to crowd them out, he is pretty sure to ask himself why that is so, and to detect and cure what is really a subtle form of self-indulgence. So then a time-table is a very necessary and useful thing. There are, however, two cautions which are worth offering. They are these:

(*a*) A time-table is not a moral law, and may be departed from without sin. If, through slackness or wilful carelessness, you have neglected the duties set down for the day, then you have sinned. But the carelessness and slackness constitute the sin, not the failure to keep to your time-table. There is no sense in making extra and unnecessary burdens for the conscience. Personally, I should never hesitate to depart from my time-table if there seemed to be any good reason for doing so. And all sense of there being anything wrong in so doing may be avoided by cultivating the habit of looking ahead, when saying one's prayers the night before or in the morning, and considering what modifications of one's daily rule the special circumstances of the day may render necessary.

(*b*) It should always be remembered that a time-table, or rule of life, is a means to an end, namely, the best and most fruitful use of one's time, and not an end in itself. It must not be allowed to become a fetish. A man who would refuse to do some obviously useful and necessary work at the only available time because his time-table said that at that time he should be in his study, or in his schools, or at his prayers, has allowed system to become his master instead of his servant, and has let his rule of life hinder, instead of helping, his work. With these few and obvious preliminary cautions, we may proceed to consider how best to order one's day.

There will usually be certain more or less fixed points in the day, such as times of church services, standing parochial engagements, and meals, which lie outside the control of an assistant curate. Within these he must find time for four things:

I. Private devotion.
II. Study.
III. Parish work.
IV. Reasonable recreation.

Let us consider each of these things in turn.

I. *Private Devotion*

(i) There is nothing at all of such vital importance to a clergyman and his work as the quantity and quality of his private prayer. All who are qualified to speak agree that there is nothing from which the Church is suffering more than from prayerlessness. I am sometimes tempted to fear that no men suffer from this more than the clergy themselves. All the most distinctively clerical faults, such as fussiness, irritability, and overbearingness are fruits of prayerlessness; and the fruit of the spirit, which is also the fruit of prayer, is 'love, joy, peace, long-suffering, gentleness, goodness, faith, meekness, self-control.' Just, in fact, the things we clergy most need and often most lack. It is not too much to say that work without prayer is worse than useless, and that to economise time at the expense of private prayer is the most fatal of all mistakes. How many mistakes we should have avoided, if we had looked ahead in prayer and guarded ourselves against the hour of temptation by prayer! There is a beautiful story of the late Archbishop Maclagan which tells how, having to preside, as rector of Newington, at a vestry meeting where he knew he would be subjected to rudeness and insult, he armed himself with a slip of paper on which he had written 'Love as brethren, be pitiful, be courteous, not rendering evil for evil or railing for railing, but contrariwise blessing,' and read it from time to time to calm his mind. One of his opponents, taking it for some secret notes, demanded that it should be passed round. This Dr. Maclagan steadily refused to do; but when a riot seemed probable he consented to show it to his chief opponent. The story gradually leaked out, and the opposition to him dwindled away.

But we have higher authority for looking ahead, and breaking the power of evil by prayer at long range, if I may use the expression, even than that of the archbishop. No one, I take it, can doubt that the battle of Calvary was fought and won in Gethsemane. That was where Christ was weak, and amazed, and beaten to the ground. And when the battle had been won there, in all the rest He is as calm, strong, and unmoved as a conqueror marching to triumph.

And as we avoid falls by prayerful looking ahead, so we garner fruits of experience by prayerful looking back on what is past. We should all of us, I suspect, make more progress in the spiritual life if we allowed forethought for the coming day and self-examination as to the day that is past to play a larger part in our daily prayers.

(ii) But this distinctively *personal* prayer must obviously form but a part of our private prayers. There must be systematic and regular intercessory prayer for our own private circle of relations, friends, benefactors, etc., for the parish, both for individuals and for societies, and for the Church at large, at home and in the mission field. Especially is detailed intercession for the parish, both for individuals and societies, valuable and necessary. It is the cure for worrying, hopelessness, and quarrelling. It is the cure for worrying, for when you can do nothing else for a person or cause you can pray, and *orare est laborare*. It is the cure for hopelessness, since prayer always stimulates one to make one more effort. It is the cure for quarrelling, since one cannot go on feeling bitter against anyone whom one has prayed for. In this connection I should like to give a rather obvious, but yet I think needed, reminder. No one remains always and at all times in one and the same frame of mind. The fact that I was awkward and ill-tempered on Monday last does not preclude the possibility of my being tractable and agreeable on Tuesday or Wednesday. This we all recognise of ourselves ; we forget to recognise it of others. A clergyman calls and finds a lad rude and stubborn, or a man cold and unresponsive, and goes away thinking that it is no use trying to do anything with such an unmannerly fellow. If he does not pray about him he will very likely leave him altogether alone for the future, and so lose him. If he prays, he decides to have another try, and perhaps to his great surprise—surprise which is at once natural and quite unreasonable—finds the man or lad tractable and pleasant. Probably he was ashamed of his rudeness even while being talked to the first time, and would have been glad to yield even then if it could have been done without too obvious a climbing down. For this and similar reasons intercessory prayer for individuals in the parish is of vital importance. So too, of course, for one's own circle and for the Church at large. Prayer is the great key to sympathy and understanding.

(iii) Along with private prayer and intercessory prayer place must be found for devotional study of Holy Scripture. We are pledged to this in the Ordinal, and reading for sermons, or Sunday school lessons, is not a substitute for directly devotional reading. Indeed, what I may call *ad hoc* study—the study, that is to say, which is undertaken in preparation for a particular sermon or lesson—is curiously fruitless of spiritual nourishment. On the other hand, the daily Bible reading which is prayed over, and the regular mediation, weekly or oftener, which is undertaken with no object beyond that of devotion, will be found indirectly most fruitful, and will yield abundant matter for sermons. For such reading truly makes us 'wise unto salvation' (2 Tim. iii. 15).

It will obviously need careful ordering of time to make room for all these things. Each man will have to find out for himself whether the morning or the evening hours are with him the most fruitful for prayer. In parishes where there is much late work in clubs and meetings, and where mattins is said early or where there is a daily Eucharist, it may be well to say very brief morning prayers and to have a set time for devotion after breakfast. Where mattins is not said till 9.30 A.M. or later, the early hours would seem the obvious time. But in any case have a fixed hour for rising. In this above all things let the flesh be subdued to the spirit. But have sleep enough. And remember that nothing is gained by putting your devotions at the most inconvenient time. But I have dealt at length with these and similar details in my book, 'Studies in the Devotional Life,' and must not repeat myself.

II. *Study*

(i) It is absolutely impossible to overrate the importance of cultivating habits of study from the very first. At my own ordination a speaker said: 'Believe me, my brothers, the day will come when, in the midst of the rush of a busy parish, you will gasp for an hour's quiet study as a drowning man gasps for air.' Doubtless this is often true, but unfortunately not always. Some clergy seem to have lost alike the power and the taste for reading. Dr. Gore is reported, I do not know whether truly or not, to have said: 'There are two kinds of bishops in England to-day: those who never read because they never have any time, and those who never read because they have long ago lost the power or desire to do so.' I fear we parochial clergy are likely to fall into a like state. Yet it cannot be too often asserted that it is quite impossible for any man to go on preaching if he does not read. You can't pour out without taking in. Once when I had preached for a friend he said to me at supper afterwards, 'I really have no time for study. I often don't touch a book for months. Sometimes I am so busy all the week that I go into church on Sunday without having had time to think what I am going to say. I often pick my text while the choir are singing the Psalms.' I felt inclined to reply, 'My dear brother, there was no need to tell me that. I knew it directly I got into the pulpit.' The people had evidently never been accustomed to be preached to. They settled themselves to sleep or to think of other things before the text was given out. An avalanche would scarcely have roused them. The late Archbishop Temple once said, 'If the time ever comes when you have to choose between study and visiting, and honestly cannot do both, choose study.' For a man who thought as highly as he did of the need for visiting, it was a remarkable thing to say. Yet, highly as I set the duty of visiting, I thoroughly agree with him. Let us then consider how best to study.

(ii) The first question is when and where to study. Different men have different methods, but I should certainly say in the morning, and in your own room. From 9 A.M. till lunch time, or, if you have day schools to open and to teach in, from 10 A.M. to lunch should be given to study. I would not say a word against such excellent societies as the J.C.M.A. and Y.C.M.U., but I always feel jealous of societies whose meetings encroach on the precious morning hours of study. I cannot help thinking that the number of mornings in each month which a clergyman, at any rate in his first few years as a parish priest, allows himself to spend outside his own study should be rigidly limited. If you make a rule to have four mornings a week of undisturbed study—leaving one week day morning for your day off and one for parochial or extra-parochial meetings—then if you want another morning for meetings it will have to be taken at the expense of your day off. A very wholesome discipline. As to meetings for united study, each man must decide for himself as to their value. Personally, I find I can get through much more by myself, in my own study, reading on my own lines, and on subjects that interest me, than I can in company with others. And there is the time wasted in going to the place of common meeting, and coming back, and the time lost by the unpunctuality of some members and the garrulity of others. But perhaps some men may find real help in such meetings. Each reader had better try for himself and see whether membership of a reading society really yields fruit. But in any case, I earnestly exhort you *to be in your own studies as many mornings a week as possible.* Reading, as Bacon says, maketh a full man.

(iii) When our hours of study are settled, the next question to be decided is what to read. It seems to me that a clergyman's reading should include three main divisions, namely:

(*a*) Theology.
(*β*) A special subject.
(*γ*) General literature.

Let us consider each of these in detail.

(*a*) Theology. What is the cause of most of the evils in our Church life to-day? Ignorance, blank ignorance. Most people know very little about the religion they profess. Many young people, both men and women, have told me that they have given up Christianity because they can no longer accept what the Church teaches. Yet when I have come to question them I have found that they really knew nothing about what the Church does teach. But they could hardly be blamed, for they had probably never been taught. Our public schools glory in neglecting doctrinal teaching. A missionary once spoke to me about having a Chinaman under instruction for baptism for over two years. Yet it is a safe thing to say that many a young Englishman passes through seven years at a big public school and three or four at the Varsity, and at the end has had less instruction in what Christianity really teaches than that Chinaman had in the first fortnight. When I was at school I spent a Sunday in the sanatorium, and a friend, a deeply thoughtful lad of eighteen with whom I often discussed serious questions, came up to see me. I asked what the sermon was about, 'Oh! the usual piffle,' he replied; 'all about being gentlemen and living in the fresh air.' Not surely an altogether unfair description of the type of religious teaching offered in many of our big public schools. And the state of our working-class lads and girls is almost—I think certainly not quite, but almost—as bad. A Roman priest once remarked to me, 'If you go into our day schools you'll not find a child over seven who can't tell you what he believes and why he believes it. Could you say the same of your schools? ' We need to realise that most of our congregations know little or nothing of the religion they profess. And therefore they need plain doctrinal teaching. And anyone who has tried the experiment will testify that there is nothing to which people respond more readily, or for which they are more grateful, than such teaching. But in how many churches is doctrinal teaching given? All my life I have been—partly owing to my mother's teaching and example, and partly owing to my own taste for such things—an indefatigable sermon taster. Yet it was some years after my ordination before I heard my first sermon on the doctrine of Holy Baptism, and then I preached it myself. But before the clergy can teach they must themselves learn. The ignorance of the clergy on matters doctrinal is a real menace to Christianity. Ask any examining chaplain what is the standard of knowledge attained by many excellent and well-meaning young men who are sent out into the parishes to instruct the laity. But we need not ask the examining chaplains to reveal the secrets of their dreadful calling. The sermons we hear week by week are witness enough. Many young High Church clergy seem to have no doctrine at all except a little semi-Roman doctrine of the Eucharist, on which they harp with little understanding till the laity are weary of it. Equally many Low Church curates reiterate one stereotyped appeal for surrender to the Holy Spirit, as if conversion were not merely the beginning but the whole of the spiritual life. What wonder that our people are not edified—

built up, that is to say, in their most holy faith—but fall ready victims to the teachings of spiritualism, theosophy, Christian science, and atheistic socialism.

The parson should therefore read theology, and read it regularly as a doctor, who desires to keep abreast of his subject, reads medicine and surgery. Firstly, we need a good general introduction which will give an outline of Christian doctrine. Christian doctrines are not separate and unconnected assertions, but parts of one coherent system of thought, of which so capable a critic as Lessing remarked that he knew nothing in the world in which human ingenuity showed and exercised itself in a greater manner. And the student should therefore study closely a good treatise on Christian dogmatics. Then he should go on to study separate doctrines in detail, taking care to read several books on each subject and to select these books from various schools of thought, so as to avoid a one-sided presentation. In this way he should read the doctrine of the Incarnation, the Atonement, the Sacraments, the work of the Holy Spirit, the Church and the Ministry, Sin, and the Intermediate and Future States. Many of these subjects may be studied historically, as in a good treatise on the Creed or the Articles, or in the history of some special period. This leads us to the thought of the study of Church history. Some men approach a subject most easily from a philosophic point of view, and they will read dogmatics with pleasure. Others find the historic method more helpful, and they will read Church history. In Church history it is a good plan to try to read everything connected with a special period. Just after my own ordination I read Church's 'History of the Oxford Movement,' and taking that as a text-book I determined to read everything I could lay my hands on connected with the Movement—tracts, sermons, memoirs, histories. I don't suppose I covered the ground, but it supplied interesting reading for three years and led me to do the same, with rather less thoroughness, with Overton's 'Evangelical Revival in the Eighteenth Century.' A book which I would cordially recommend to all students of Church history is Rufus Jones' 'Studies in Mystical Religion,' which if followed up with keenness should supply subjects of study for years.

The study of doctrine and Church history must always go hand in hand with the study of Holy Scripture. It is an excellent thing to keep a good commentary on some book of the New Testament at hand, *in cut*, if I may use the expression, and to study a chapter, or even a few verses, when you have any spare time. Nothing is so fruitful of ideas for sermons as a morning spent, with no thought of sermons, over Westcott's 'Hebrews,' or Lightfoot's 'Galatians,' or Sanday and Headlam's 'Romans.' For most of us, especially those who like myself know no Hebrew, it is not possible to treat the Old Testament with equal thoroughness. But we ought not to let any obscure passage in the daily lessons pass us without seeing if a good commentary can throw any light, nor ought we to rest content while any book, or any writer, in the Old Testament has no meaning or lesson for us. Such a book as Kirkpatrick's 'Doctrine of the Prophets' is obviously a help, and Macmillan's

'One Volume Commentary' (ed. Dummelow) supplies good introductions to the study of all the books. For the period between the close of the Old Testament and the opening of the New I have found no book more interesting than 'The Background of the Gospels,' by W. Fairweather, and it has led me on to further interesting reading, which is the real test of the value of a book.

In all your Bible study I would advise you to have an interleaved Bible handy, and to put into it any ideas of special value. But do not be in a hurry to put things in, for even the most generously interleaved Bible quickly fills. Make your notes in a notebook, and only put the cream of your notebooks into your Bible.

The Bible itself, doctrine, and Church history are obviously the main subjects of theological study, and it is impossible for me, within the narrow limits of these lectures, to go into further detail. But the man who really loves study will be sure to specialise, and there are unnumbered subjects which are interesting in themselves, and which will enrich preaching and help in parish work. The philosophy of religion, and comparative religion, the history of Christian mysticism —which will supply interesting reading for a lifetime—liturgiology, ecclesiastical art, the history of monasticism, and a thousand and one other subjects and sections of subjects. Let a man once get the love for study and he will never lose it.

(β) The last words of the last paragraph suggest the second division of our reading, namely, a man's own subject. Professor Marshall of Cambridge, my deep debt to whom I am glad to have this opportunity of gratefully acknowledging, said to me when I left Cambridge: 'Don't lose all intellectual interests in your new parish. Don't let life be bounded on the north by the mother's meeting and on the south by the lad's club. Choose a subject and read it. It will keep you fresh and sweet.' And I know how much I owe to trying to follow that advice. So have a subject—history, natural science, philosophy, ethics, sociology, or what not. Take in the *Quarterly Journal* of your subject, and try to keep abreast of what is going on in it. Plan to write a book on it. It does not much matter if the book is never written. The reading, the thinking, the mental aliveness is what matters. A little while ago a candidate for deacon's orders, who had taken a good degree in history, told me that as soon as he was settled in his parish he meant to start reading, so as to find out 'all there is to be known about the Church of the first five centuries.' It is hardly likely that he will succeed, but I am sure he and his work will be all the better for the attempt. No matter how remote a man's special subject may be from theology, it will enrich his preaching and benefit his work. Most will naturally select their special subject from those they studied for their degree.

(γ) Along with theological reading, which should never be discontinued, and the reading of one's special subject, which no man is likely to drop when once he has given himself to it seriously, every clergyman should try to keep up his general reading—travels, biography, essays, poetry, and the best fiction. I fear many young clergy will think I am setting an unattainably high standard, but it is just as easy—and when the taste for it has been gained, far pleasanter—to read good literature as to read the *Strand Magazine* or the novels of Mr. Charles Garvice. There is an easy and natural way of gaining a taste for travels and biography, namely, by taking a special part of the mission field, say India, South or Central Africa, the Pacific Islands, or what not, and reading up the history, biographies, and chief books of travel and sport connected with it. I have at different times tried this plan with North-West India and with South Africa and found it most interesting. Poetry, like music, is, I suspect, a taste which, while it can be cultivated or neglected, is either born in a man or denied him. Some men seem constitutionally incapable of reading it. But it adds immensely to a man's preaching power and to his general culture, and a real love for poetry supplies, among the thousand little worries of daily work,

> 'A shadowy isle of bliss
> Midmost the beating of the steely sea.'

I know a business man, head of a great bank, who keeps a small volume of good selections on his bedroom mantlepiece and learns a few verses as he dresses and undresses. And one of the most effective parish priests I know is acquainted with the literature of the eighteenth century to an extent that a college professor might envy.

Professor Saintsbury's books, Mr. Birrell's delightful essays, Mr. Leslie Stephen's 'Hours in a Library, the volumes of the 'English Men of Letters' series, and similar works set one reading for oneself, and make the present cheap reprints of the best English literature a real joy. Nor should really good novels be neglected, whether the classics such as Fielding, Richardson, Jane Austen, Thackeray, and the rest or the best men writing to-day.

But along whatever lines one's general reading may lie, it is our clear duty to aim at what I can only call, for lack of a better expression, general culture. For in the midst of multifarious duties there lurks for all of us this dreadful fate, to lose the power of serious study and the enjoyment of anything but trashy reading.

III. *Parochial Work*

(i) The third place on our daily time-table must be given to parochial work—services, schools, visiting, clubs and meetings, and secretarial work. These are a barren waste of time without prayer, and so take a lower place than a man's own private devotions. And they must not be allowed to encroach at all on the time given to theological study, nor to crowd out even lighter and more general reading altogether. On the other hand, it is these things which constitute what, in the eyes of the world, is our real work, and it is for these that prayer and study are the necessary preparation. Now while a man is an assistant curate, and not himself vicar or rector of a parish, the times of the services and school lessons will probably be settled for him. These then, with meal times, may be taken as fixed points round which the day is ordered and arranged. Now as, speaking generally, the mornings should be kept as much as possible for study, and the number of mornings per month devoted to anything else strictly limited, so, broadly speaking, the afternoons should be devoted to visiting, and the number of afternoons which we allow to be taken from this duty for the sake of attending meetings should be severely limited. There may be, of course, special parishes where local conditions make some different arrangement necessary. But I am writing of ordinary parish work. I would therefore recommend every young curate to have a rule, not merely as to the number of hours visiting which he does per week, but also as to the time at which he lays aside his after-dinner pipe and newspaper and starts visiting. I shall hope to treat in some detail of parochial visiting in the next chapter, so I need not say more at present than that the bulk of our afternoons, and some time in the evenings, should be given to this work. The ordering of one's evenings is perhaps the most difficult part of the whole task of forming a time-table. But this I would say. Do not at first be anxious to fill up every moment of the week. If you find yourself with empty time on your hands, it is always easy to put in an extra hour's study or visiting; but if at first you let every evening be filled with its club, or guild, or meeting, then as work develops you will find yourself unable to do justice to any one of a thousand competing duties. There are several things, obvious in themselves yet easily forgotten, which young men just starting work would do well to remember. One is that when once a thing is started it has to be kept up. Nothing has a worse effect, alike on you and your workers, than the starting of organisations which soon languish and come to nothing. So do not be in a hurry to fill every hour of your time-table. Leave a margin over for unforeseen developments. Another thing worth remembering is, that one thing thoroughly done is worth five things scamped.

(ii) This last thought suggests the need of business method in our parochial work, and therefore of the need for finding a place in our time-table for secretarial work. There are letters to be written, registers to be filled up, accounts to be kept, notices to be cyclostyled and sent out, and a quantity of other things to be done for which a business man would have a clerk, or many clerks. Much is lost if we keep no record of our visiting, no register of the attendance at Communion, at least of our boys and girls if not all communicants,[1] no notes for reference in future years. Yet these things cannot be attended to without the expenditure of time. And I hope I shall not be thought to be descending to subjects unworthy of a lecturer in pastoral theology if I say that a small set of lettered cabinets with drawers, marked 'Sick and Poor,' 'Confirmation Candidates,' 'Personal,' 'Guild,' 'Sunday School,' 'Mission,' etc., an indexed note-book or two, a well-posted address-book, and even a copying-press and letter-book for your more important letters, will be found of great value, and will in the end save much time. The chaos of too many clerical studies cannot be conducive to good or rapid work,

[1] See *infra*, pp. 213–214.

and thirty shillings spent on office furniture, files, notebooks, cabinets, etc., goes a long way. Finally, I would say that some good multiplying machine—personally I recommend the neo-cyclostyle as the cheapest, cleanest, and most convenient—is of infinite use for reproducing notices, notes of addresses, Sunday school lessons, and a thousand similar things.

IV. *Recreation*

(i) I am afraid I have painted rather a terrifying picture of a clergyman's day and of the claims on his time. I am glad, therefore, to end this first chapter by speaking of recreation. And this is almost as important a subject as any I have yet touched on. For no man can live or ought to live without recreation. On the other hand if, when one is playing, or resting, or reading for one's own enjoyment, one's conscience is reproaching one, and one feels obliged, if found so doing by a visitor, to excuse oneself for not being at work, all the value of recreation is lost. What, then, should be one's rule of recreation. Let us consider it under two heads, namely, daily recreation and one's day off a week.

(ii) Every day should find time for some recreation. A short time on the sofa after one's midday meal, say from 1.45, if dinner finishes by that time, to 2.30 P.M., when one starts the afternoon's work, is good for body and mind. A similar rest with a pipe and a light book before starting the evening's work is a good thing. Then there is the daily paper. I am sure we all waste a lot of time over newspapers which might be much better spent. I would not recommend anyone to follow my example, for I think it was a mistake, but for more than ten years after my ordination I took neither morning nor evening paper, and did not often see one. But though this was, I think, a mistake, I am sure we need rule and discipline with regard to newspapers. If, for instance, a man living alone in lodgings will take one daily paper, say a morning one, instead of two, and at tea, in place of reading an evening paper, will read history (Froude, Macaulay, Justin McCarthy's 'Reign of Queen Anne,' 'History of the Four Georges,' and 'William IV,' and 'History of our Own Times'), memoirs, and diaries (Pepys, Evelyn's Diary, Walpole's Letters, Boswell's Johnson), essays (Macaulay, Leslie Stephen, Froude, Bagehot, Birrell), and contemporary biographies and travels, he will lose little and gain much. Dr. Gibson, when Principal of Leeds Clergy School, used to recommend men not to read the daily paper till after dinner. It is an excellent rule. If, however, you read it at breakfast, put it aside rigidly at a fixed hour. It is wonderful what a difference it makes to your morning's reading whether you start punctually at 9 A.M. or at a quarter to ten, when three-quarters of an hour have been frittered away over a paper. And a similar caution is needed about that last delightful half-hour before going to bed. No man can do without his proper allowance of sleep, and there is more self-indulgence shown in sitting up too late dawdling time away with a novel than in almost any way. Find time in your daily plan of life for the daily paper, the hour's light reading, social intercourse with friends, or even for pure undiluted slacking, but see that all these things are kept within bounds.

(iii) A day off a week is an absolute necessity, at any rate for a man under forty. As a man grows older, and needs less active exercise than when young, and as his work develops in variety and interest, so that one piece of work is the relaxation and rest needed after some other piece, a day off each week may become less necessary. But young men should always get it. Clearly it is the duty of a vicar not merely to allow each of his curates a day off, but to see that he gets it. One of the best parish priests I know, the head of a large staff, will not allow one of his curates even to attend a service in church on his day off. If a man really thinks it necessary, he says, to attend church every single day of the week, he can go to some neighbouring church on his day off. The result is that if a man takes, let us say, Tuesday off, he is absolutely free from the time he goes to bed on Monday till he gets up on Wednesday. He can lie a little late on Tuesday morning—and one late morning a week is not bad for anyone—and when he gets back from a day's golf or cycling he has not got to spoil it all by turning out for an evening's work in the lad's club or schools. On the other hand, I have known a curate in a specially hard and depressing parish, whose day off began after the midday intercessions in church, and ended in time for evensong and the evening's work; and even then, he says, he only managed to secure it about once in two months. What wonder that a bad breakdown resulted from such folly. And I feel bound to add that inquiries which I have made among ordination candidates up for priest's orders—inquiries made in quite a number of dioceses—make me fear that many curates do not get a weekly holiday. Do not therefore hesitate to insist on your day off. If your vicar seems to think you unreasonable on the point, show him this paragraph.

On the question of what are, and what are not, suitable recreations for a clergyman, I have written at some length elsewhere.[1] Here I will only say that any recreation which is suitable for a decent layman seems equally suitable for a decent clergyman. As long as one is careful not to let recreation encroach on one's times for work, I think the Church and the individual alike have much to gain by clergy joining freely in games and going to theatres and the better-class music-halls.

One question of a practical nature has been put to me several times and may well be touched on here. Often when a curate is a fine athlete he is asked to play for the local cricket or football team. By so doing he is brought into contact with many men whom he might otherwise not meet, and has opportunities of commending religion, without a word spoken yet in a very real and practical way, to many people. Should the Saturday spent playing cricket or football with the local team count as a curate's day off or as work? It is impossible to give a general answer to this question. If the bulk of the players are drawn from the clergyman's own parish, I do not think it unreasonable to count the afternoon's game as real parish work. If

[1] 'How to Deal with Men.' E. Arnold.

the team is a first-class one drawn from a large district, and one of which few members are, or are likely to become, members of one's own church, I think a curate should either not play for it or regard such playing as his own recreation. At any rate I am sure a vicar would be justified in saying, 'I am afraid we can't spare two afternoons a week from the parish as a regular thing. If you want to play regularly for the Rovers, it must count as your day off.'

Annual Events

(i) Hitherto we have been considering the normal arrangement of your time from day to day. But there are some things which are, I think, worth saying about the annual holiday. It is a good thing, when possible, to get a few days, say Monday to Saturday, off before Lent or after Easter. After all, such holidays are reasonable as a set-off against the holidays which a business man gets at Christmas and Easter, and the greater freedom of his week-ends. But do not be always running away for 'just a few days off in the country.' You would not do it if you were a doctor, a lawyer, a banker, or a merchant. And the way in which some clergy will say that if they can get baptisms and the mid-week sermon arranged for there is no reason why they should not get away, simply confirms the laity in their belief that the parson's job is, if not a one day a week job, at any rate a very easy one.

The summer holiday is, however, quite a different matter, and I am sure a man owes it to himself, or indeed to his congregation, to take one every year, except in very exceptional circumstances. In one parish in which I worked the rule was that each member of the staff was allowed four Sundays in the year. He might take these altogether, which gave him practically five weeks, or he might divide his holiday in two, but not more than two, parts, which gave him practically six weeks. This I consider very liberal. Personally, I think there are many reasons for taking the four Sundays all at once. It gives, as I have said, practically five clear weeks, which with one or more short Monday to Saturday holidays should be enough for any busy man. One thoroughly good holiday is, I believe, a better rest than two shorter ones. It interferes less with work, and it gives the laity less reason for complaining that the clergy are 'always going away for holidays.' But this is a detail which every man must settle for himself.

When you take a holiday let it be a real one. Some men, for financial or other reasons, have to take a job as *locum tenens*, but it is always a pity that it should be necessary. If you are in charge of a parish the absent vicar may have assured you that nothing will be required but the Sunday services, but there are sure to be other claims—funerals, baptisms, sick cases needing visiting, and similar things which can hardly be neglected. But if you are in a constant state of conflict between your natural, and quite laudable, desire to enjoy a good holiday and the whisperings of conscience, much of the good of your holiday will be lost.

I would also advise you to be adamant in your

refusal to preach while on holiday. Many clergy are quite shameless in the claims they make on the help of visitors. Quite recently a clergyman gave me no peace with his urgent requests that I would preach for him during my holiday in his parish. He said his people so seldom had a chance to hear any voice but his, and it would be a spiritual refreshment to them. As a matter of fact he got, if I may believe what my host told me, one or both of his Sunday sermons preached for him by visitors three Sundays out of four from the beginning of May to the end of September. If you are spending all, or part, of your holiday at home, where you were brought up, many people will no doubt be glad to hear you, and if you preach an old sermon it will be no great sacrifice of time. But personally I like my holiday to be a spiritual refreshment to myself. It is a great opportunity to hear other men preach, to visit interesting churches, and to worship free from care or responsibility.

(ii) Speaking of a holiday as a spiritual refreshment suggests another subject which it may be well to touch on. Before you go on your holiday draw up for yourself a special holiday rule of devotion, meditation and prayer, and church-going. It is not likely that your ordinary one will be suitable. Your holiday one need not be so strict, and the times and hours will almost certainly want alteration. But when you have not got the helps supplied in the parish by regular services, necessary Bible study, and an ordered daily time-table, some rule of life becomes more and not less necessary. It is a poor thing to return from a holiday physically strengthened and spiritually weakened. Nor, to put the matter on the lowest grounds, will it help the laity to see a clergyman who is very strict about church-going in his own parish yet on his holiday reduces his religious duties to the barest possible minimum. So sketch a rule of life, or perhaps I ought to say an ideal of life, before you go on your holiday, reserving to yourself the right to modify it, for sufficient reasons, to meet the claims of others with whom you are living.

One suggestion may seem to many a counsel of perfection, but I am sure it is worth offering. Set yourself a holiday task. Take some good solid book for holiday reading. There are sure to be wet days, or days when time for one reason or another hangs heavy. And quite apart from this, if you are climbing or sailing, playing golf or tennis, or going excursions all the afternoon and enjoying social pleasures all the evening, a couple of hours' study or serious reading in the morning will add to, rather than detract from, the pleasure of the day. And it is pleasant, when holidays are over, to find that you have broken the back of some piece of really stiff reading, and have returned to work keener, rather than less keen, on serious study.

I learned this lesson on the way back from South Africa. The voyage took eighteen days, and each day I smoked a pipe or played a couple of games of deck quoits after breakfast, and then settled down to three hours steady work in the saloon. This left all the afternoon and evening for novel reading, deck games, social intercourse, concerts, and pleasant loafing.

As we drew near Southampton a friend asked me if I were not bored to death with the voyage, and if I should not be glad to be on land again. 'Good heavens, no!' I said. 'I wish the captain would remember he had forgotten something at Cape Town and turn back to get it, so that I might have five weeks more.' The man seemed so astonished that I decided to ask some of the other passengers. I found all bored and weary of the voyage. If they had mingled solids with the sweets of idleness, they would all have enjoyed the voyage more. I think the same is true of holidays.

(iii) I must not end this chapter without a word about the value of an annual retreat. I cannot write fully on the subject, as I have treated it in a chapter I contributed to a book on the subject of Retreats. But I do not think the value of an annual retreat can possibly be exaggerated. I have known many clergy who shrank from them. I have never known one who, having attended one, did not declare that he would try and get one a year, or at least one every two years, as long as he lived. And generally speaking a long retreat, say from Monday or Tuesday evening to Saturday morning, is beyond all comparison more helpful and valuable than a short one of only one or two clear days. And a strict retreat, in which silence is observed, except perhaps during the afternoon walk, is far more helpful, and if a man sets his mind to it far pleasanter, than a lax one. So deeply convinced am I of the value of retreats that I would urge every clergyman to use them, even if the time for one has to be deducted from his holidays. But as retreats for clergy are always arranged so as not to include a Sunday, most vicars will be able, and should be willing, to allow their curates time for a retreat in addition to the annual holiday.

If a proper retreat is absolutely impossible, there is a useful alternative. I have long been of opinion that the addresses, no matter how helpful, are the least valuable part of a retreat, and that it is the silence, the freedom from interruptions and worries, and the opportunities for prayer and thought that are the chief things. If therefore you can't get to a public retreat, have a one-day retreat of your own in your own church, or in a neighbouring church where there is a daily celebration or a weekday celebration on a day that suits you. Go to the Holy Communion; arrange to have breakfast by yourself, and read a devotional book instead of the newspaper; spend the morning in reviewing and praying over your own devotional life and revising your rules of prayer and study; have dinner by yourself, and devote the afternoon to revision and prayer in connection with your rule of visiting and parish work; have tea by yourself, and spend the rest of the time in prayer, meditation, and intercession in connection with the various points of failure, or encouragement and of hope suggested during the day; finally, go to bed early. There are obvious advantages in using your own church, since it is easy to arrange for meals in your lodgings or the Clergy House. But a strange church has its advantages, since you are freer from interruptions, and if you know the vicar and tell him beforehand that you are proposing so to use his church, he will generally see that you are undisturbed. But don't accept his kind offers of meals in the vicarage. Rather arrange at the nearest inn for meals at such times as you can have them at a separate table or in a room by yourself.

One thing is much to be desired, namely, that there should be a large churchyard or walled vicarage garden, where if the day is fine you can walk up and down as you pray and meditate. For many people find such walking a great help to quiet thought.

CHAPTER II

PAROCHIAL VISITING

Systematic Visiting: (i) Its too frequent neglect; (ii) A poor excuse for that neglect; (iii) A more reasonable excuse.
House-to-house Visiting: (i) Its object—sympathetic knowledge; (ii) Its necessity as a missionary effort; (iii) Sick, poor, and impotent folk.
Method of Visiting: (i) Preparation of a visiting-book; (ii) Getting into houses; (iii) Notes in one's day-book; (iv) Return visits; (v) Prayer when visiting.
Special Visiting: (i) Boys; (ii) Men; (iii) Lapsed communicants and Confirmation candidates; (iv) Absentees.
Sick Visiting: (i) Dying cases; (ii) The Visitation Office; (iii) Long illness; (iv) Chronic cases; (v) Hospital visiting.
General Remarks: (i) Revisiting a district; (ii) Picking up a lost habit.

(i) The next subject which must engage our attention is how best to get into close personal touch with our people. Our Blessed Lord gives us the true ideal of the pastor in the words, 'I know My sheep and am known of Mine.' The most regular, careful, and beautiful services, the most eloquent and thoughtful preaching the most elaborate music, not one or all of these things will supply the lack of that true pastoral relationship which nothing but personal knowledge of your people will give. I am convinced that the old saying, 'A house-going parson makes a church-going people' is true. Every now and then, when the subject crops up in the correspondence columns of church newspapers, you will find it stated that poor people resent the visits of the clergy and regard them as impertinent and inquisitorial. If visits are ever so regarded it must, I should think, be due to some fatal mistake in manner or spirit on the part of the visitor. But I can truthfully say that in twenty years' experience in London and the country, in North and South, I have never met a single example of any such feeling. On the other hand, I have met, I am sure, many hundreds of examples where regular visiting has been mentioned with enthusiasm as one of the virtues of some popular clergyman, or failure to visit complained of as a fault. How often does one hear the complaint: 'I've been in this house so many years and no clergyman has called,' or again, 'Oh! I've been to his church often enough but no one called to see me'? Rightly or wrongly, English people are deeply convinced that the clergy ought to visit. And personally I think that this instinct is a right one. For the duty of the pastor is not to wait till the sheep come to him, but to go after the sheep, and to go after them till he find them. No doubt the instinct that the clergy ought to visit is often displayed by the laity in an unreasonable form. People will absent themselves from church for years, and then complain bitterly that no clergyman called when some one whom the clergyman had never seen or heard of was ill for a fortnight, or suppose that the clergy ought to know by instinct that a year old baby has died, 'because it was christened at your church last November.' But only very young men will expect their fellow-creatures to display reason, and the unreasonableness of others is no excuse for neglecting one's own duty. Let us consider briefly some reasons why it is often neglected by junior clergy.

(ii) One reason for the neglect of visiting by some of the junior clergy is, I suspect, because they think that their seniors, while keen that junior clergy should visit, yet neglect it themselves. Now, though of course there may be vicars and rectors who neglect visiting without excuse, yet I would beg all young men not hastily to decide that their seniors are careless in the matter. As a man gets on in years and experience, and gets caught up in the network of ruri-decanal, diocesan, and general church business, he inevitably spends time in administrative work which would once have been spent in house-to-house visiting. A clergyman, now a diocesan bishop, said to me when I was in my first curacy, 'Ah, Green, you are lucky. You can still keep in touch with human beings. My life is swamped in committees, and committees have no souls.' And even so many a busy vicar or rector does sick and special visiting of which his curates may know nothing. At any rate, visiting does not cease to be a good thing because some one else neglects it. Get the taste for it young and you will not lose it.

(iii) Another and more important reason for neglect of visiting is that it is undertaken in an unintelligent and unsystematic manner which accentuates its difficulties and prevents its yielding much fruit, and so the curate who has perhaps begun with the best intentions gets discouraged and soon joins the ranks of those who tell you that they don't believe in visiting, and think that it is a waste of time and energy. And for this there is really much excuse. Visiting people of whom one knows nothing is a difficult task at the best of times. For a young, inexperienced, and nervous curate, quite ignorant of the parish, and making perhaps his first acquaintance with working-class people, it is doubly hard. One needs all the help of a right method and point of view. Yet many clergy have no instruction in the matter and no help. They are just pitchforked into a district and told to visit it. Naturally they do not feel able to go down a long line of red-brick cottages saying at each door, ' Please I've come. I am Mr. Jones, the new curate.' Let us therefore consider the object of house-to-house visiting and its method. We can then go on to consider those special forms of visiting which spring out of it, or which are demanded by special conditions and types of work.

House-to-House Visiting

(i) What, then, is the ideal, the object, of house-to-house visiting ? Undoubtedly it is a sympathetic understanding of your people. How can you preach to people of whose life and habits and thoughts you are ignorant ? And such intimate and sympathetic knowledge is only to be gained by visiting the homes. We are often told, and I believe told quite truly, that the standard of preaching is higher among Nonconformists than among Anglicans. But though I believe it to be true, yet I cannot help thinking that the parochial system, and the habit of pastoral visitation by the clergy themselves, give our preaching a spiritual value which makes up for some lack of eloquence and of wide reading. One never, I think, has a really good week's visiting without feeling the effects in the next Sunday's preaching. And for this there is an excellent reason. A very old and very wise woman once said to a young man, 'My dear, never marry a girl till you have seen her in her own home and against the background of her own family. That's the place to learn what she is really like.' Somewhat similar advice may be given to preachers. See your people against the background of their own homes, for that is the place to know them. I may illustrate this perhaps by a personal reminiscence. When first I went to one parish I had in my Bible Class a lad of about sixteen years old, who nearly turned my hair grey with his behaviour. He was utterly silly, unmanageable, and ill-behaved. I had serious thoughts of turning him out of the class, for he disturbed me and seemed a bad influence among the others. But I determined first to have a good talk with the mother, whom I had once failed to find in, and once found too busy washing to talk to me. When I did get an interview her conversation was one long song of praise of 'our Abram.' He made the fire in the morning and brought her up a cup of tea before he went to work. He did all the scrubbing, and 'wouldn't let me go on my knees to scrub a bit of board if it was ever so, along of my bad leg.' He was the only one who could do anything with his father when he was in drink, and it was always for him that his little invalid sister with hip disease used to cry when she was fretful and in pain. And with eight younger brothers and sisters, and he the only one working, he brought home not only his wages but every penny of his overtime and tips. What wonder that the unnatural strain of home gave place outside to wild, awkward, silly outbursts of spirits. But of course when I understood what a jewel 'our Abram' was, it was easy to have patience and make allowances. And as soon as the boy felt I was trying to understand him, he tried to understand me. *Tout comprendre, c'est tout pardonner.*

Or, again, it may well be that among your Sunday School teachers there will be a girl, pretty, ladylike, and refined, but who strikes you as affected, needlessly touchy, or unnecessarily scrupulous and faddy. If you find such a girl, as I have done in more than one case, the daughter of drunken parents, living in a house always noisy, always dirty, always overrun with a swarm of ragged and mannerless children, you will think less of the little sillinesses, affectations, and whims, and wonder more at the innate refinement and love for what is good, which can keep a girl steady in such a home.

And though all cases will not be of this extreme character, yet all cases will have this in common, namely, that they must be understood if any good is to be done with them, and that the key to a right understanding is the home.

(ii) I have put sympathetic understanding as the first object of house-to-house visiting, because it seems to me the most important thing of all. But there is another and more obvious one. House-to-house visiting is the chief of *missionary* efforts in a parish. In church and Sunday school you can deal with those who are willing to come to church of their own accord. Visiting is the only thing that will bring you into contact with those who do not come of their own accord, but may be induced to do so if rightly handled. And even when those you visit do not ever come to church your time has not been wasted. At the worst you have 'delivered your soul' (Ezek. iii. 19). But more than this may well have been accomplished. People who are visited will send for you in case of sickness, will be more regular in sending their children, and will help to produce in the parish a spirit of friendliness to the church. And who knows what more may be effected in their own souls?

(iii) Finally, house-to-house visitation is necessary if we are to get at those people who in some ways need the services of the Church most, and to shepherd whom is the special duty, and glory, of the Church of England. In every poor artisan parish there are old people, army pensioners, derelict old maids, chronic invalids, and other examples of the flotsam and jetsam of human nature whose lives can be immensely bettered and brightened, at no financial cost, by the kindly sympathy and spiritual ministrations of the Church. Many such people will never make the first move by themselves seeking out the Church or the clergy. They fear to be suspected by their landlady or neighbours of cadging for help (church-creeping, as it

peculiarities, and it is as well to try and learn them. When you have thoroughly spied out the land select a suitable street. Let us call it Henshaw Street, after the first I visited. Take a penny notebook of a convenient size, that is to say, as big as will slip easily into your pocket. Divide each page, by horizontal lines, into three or four divisions and number them 1, 3, 5, 7, etc., Henshaw Street, and then 2, 4, 6, etc., for the other side of the street. If your preliminary inquiries have led you to expect three families in each house, mark your spaces 1*a*, 1*b*, 1*c*, 3*a*, 3*b*, 3*c*, etc. The object is to have a space ready for notes about each family, and to avoid confusion. Then go through any parochial lists you can lay your hands on—the Communicants' roll, the Sunday school registers, the Mothers' Meeting book, etc., and wherever you find a Henshaw Street name enter it in your visiting-book in the correct space. It is not merely an advantage, when knocking at No. 19, to know that the name is Smith. It may prevent great offence, for if the woman is a regular communicant, a pillar of the Mothers' Meeting, has a boy in the choir and two girls in the Guild, and has perhaps been eagerly expecting 'the new curate' for weeks, she may be deeply hurt if you not only ask her name but go on to ask if she goes anywhere. Of course such an attitude is wholly unreasonable, but as I have already said, one must not look for reason in all one's fellow-creatures. So get all the names you can. If you have day schools ask to be allowed to look at the registers for the names of children living in Henshaw Street, or even ask a friendly head teacher to make you out a list of such children.[1] Where you have names and a few facts to go on, it is comparatively easy to pay a visit. You merely knock and say, 'Are you Mrs. Smith? Good afternoon; I am the new curate. I know your boy Willie in the choir, and of course I want to make your acquaintance. May I come in?' But there will, of course, be many houses in each street from which no members attend any church organisation at all. You may get the names of occupiers of such houses from neighbours, or from old lists of voters such as are hung up on church doors; but the mere name, if you get nothing else, is hardly worth troubling about. Let us consider how to deal with such cases.

(ii) First of all be warned against visiting all the houses in the street from which any church members come first, leaving the non-church-goers' houses last. For many reasons it is better, when visiting house to house, to take the whole street in regular order. When then you come to a house where you know no one knock boldly, and when the woman comes to the door introduce yourself by saying, 'I am the new curate at the church, and I have called as I want to make the acquaintance of everyone in my district.' If a child comes to the door say, 'Is the lady of the house in? Will you ask her to speak with me.' Now remember this; you want *to get into the house*, and it is your business to leave no stone unturned to effect this.

[1] I need hardly say that such kindly help should always be asked as a favour and accepted as a kindness. It is no part of the teacher's *duty* to help our parish work, and we have no right to demand it.

In the North I have never been ill-received. In London, people have sometimes been anxious to get rid of me, and once or twice, not oftener, but once or twice, they have been rude. It is not a bad thing, in order to gain time for a parley, unobtrusively to put a foot over the threshold. If a woman says she is too busy to be bothered, say pleasantly that you are sorry to have troubled her and will call again. And take care that you do call again soon, and to that end make a note in your visiting-book, 'Woman busy, call again.' If the woman tells you that she is a dissenter, or attends some other church, make it quite clear that you do not wish to take anyone away from where they are attending, but say that you would like to call as a friend. You will often find that the membership of chapel or of the other church is purely imaginary. The woman did not mean to say anything that was not true, but really she may not have been for years anywhere. Or, if she goes, there may be boys or girls or a husband who go nowhere. A friendly visit will do no harm, and may do good. If, however, you are told that the people of the house are Roman Catholics, it is, I think, better not to call. The people don't desire it, and the priests object to it. In such cases I always pass the time of day if anyone is standing at the door, or make a friendly remark in any time of sickness, or trouble, or family rejoicing. But they prefer to be left alone, and their wishes should be respected. Many of the women who come to the door are, however, likely to be nothing in particular in religious matters. After a few minutes of conversation you should say, 'May

I come in for a few minutes if you are not too busy ?' A visit is a failure if you do not cross the threshold. You will often be told, 'There, I'm all upset. The house is not fit to be seen,' but that is a merely formal excuse, and can be met with an apology on your part for coming when she is busy. When you are in, the great thing is to get the greatest amount of information without seeming to be asking too many questions. Fortunately, most English women of the working classes talk freely, especially about their husbands and children. Do not, on your part, be afraid of talking about yourself and your home. A friendly interchange of information promotes good feeling. One woman in my first parish discovered a great bond of union between us in the fact that I was born in Hampshire and she in Wiltshire. She often referred to it in conversation as a humorous and delightful coincidence, and when I met her again some years after leaving the parish, she spoke of it at once. One question should always be asked, namely, has she any boys of working age 'going nowhere' whom you might visit in the evening and invite to the Bible Class. Many women seem to lose all control over their children, especially the boys, when they begin to earn wages, and are only too grateful to anyone who will take an interest in them. Many other questions can be skilfully introduced according to the subjects she may be talking about. Thus a description of her young days in a country village suggests the question whether she went to church and was confirmed. The statement that she and her husband have recently moved from the other side of the town gives a natural opening for the question, 'Where used you to attend before you left there?' The thing to be avoided is a string of bald questions suggesting the census man.

(iii) From time to time during your conversation, you may get a reasonable opportunity of making notes. Thus if she has a boy of sixteen who 'used to go to Sunday school but has got broke off,' you can ask his name, where he works, and what time he gets home, and add, 'I'll just make a note to remind me to call some evening and catch him before he goes out again.' And then you can make rapid notes of many other things besides Sam and his hours of work. But if you don't get such a chance the notes must be made when you leave, in the shadow of a friendly doorway, or anywhere where you won't be seen. It is fatal to trust to even the best memory to record all the impressions of three hours' visiting among strangers where every house looks alike. And, if you have not the precious gift of remembering faces, make notes to remind you who is who. I turned out my first visiting-book the other day, and found such notes as these:

No. 26. Mrs. W——. Little red-headed woman. Squints. Ch.; but goes to chapel 'along of me husband.' Sam, 16 yrs., used to go to chapel Sunday school. Won't go now. Home about 6 o'clock.

No. 28. Mrs. H——. Stout woman in a temper, but friendly after a bit. Husband a bricklayer. Confirmed in Huntingdonshire, but not gone to Communion for years. Three children school age, two daughters working.

No. 30. Strict Baptists. Would rather I didn't call. Apparently very decent people.

No. 33. Mrs. S——. 'Milly Barton.' Seven children under 12. Husband drinks. Visit him. Children go nowhere. No clothes.

The mystic entry 'Milly Barton' was to remind me of her appearance, that I might know her again. She was like the description of Mrs. Barton in 'Scenes of Clerical Life,' a large, fair, gentle mother of many children.

Such notes need to be written out in full in a permanent register, but it is as well not to write up your day-book, as we may call it, into your ledger till you have paid several visits and know as much as possible about the family.

(iv) What I have said about paying several visits suggests my next point. Go again as soon as possible, even if you have to leave some other street wholly unvisited. It is better to visit forty houses three times than one hundred and twenty houses once. For very likely some of the women may have been much pleased and interested with your visit. If you do not go again for months—and it will take many months to get right round a big district when allowance is made for necessary sick visiting and special cases—all this interest will have evaporated, even if the women are not offended and disappointed. Now in some ways, of course, the second visit is less difficult than the first, but in some ways it is more so. On the first visit you have the advantage of the obvious motive of having called to introduce yourself. On the second visit this motive is lacking, and you must therefore invent a motive. A good opening, when you are again seated in a woman's kitchen, is, 'I've been thinking, Mrs. Smith, about what you told me when I was here last.' One woman, perhaps, told you of a neighbour who was ill and asked you to call. She may be asked to let you know of any cases of sickness in the street. Another expressed pious horror at a neighbour who had two children unbaptized, remarking, 'I mayn't be much of a church-goer myself, but I'd be ashamed to have a great boy of two and him not christened.' She should be asked to let you know, in a friendly way, of any women who are confined, so that you can call at once and suggest the bringing of the child to baptism. A third may have mentioned that 'They're new-comers at number fifteen.' She should be asked to keep an eye on the street for removals and to let you know at once, so that you may call on the new arrivals as soon as possible. You point out to her, feelingly, what a bad effect it produces if no clergyman calls for weeks and weeks after new-comers have moved in, pointing out at the same time how impossible it is for you to know all that is going on in your district. If another woman has mentioned that her old mother down in Herefordshire has been ill, it will produce a very good effect if you call a week after 'just to ask if you have heard from Herefordshire, and to hear how your mother is.' All this, written down in cold blood, seems like catching your people by guile. But try it. A boy just leaving school and going to work who may be seen and given good advice, an out-of-work brother who has joined the army and who may be written to at his depôt, or whose chaplain may be written to, a member of the family in hospital who may be visited, and a thousand other such openings for friendly interest may be and should be utilised. In a word, when you have called, find an early excuse to call a second and third time. After that a flying word as you pass the open door may be all that is possible for months at a time.

(v) There is one question which is so often asked me, and which is in itself so important, that I feel a paragraph must be devoted to it. Young clergy often say, Should I pray at every visit? On the one hand, there seems something almost unseemly in asking a busy woman, in the middle of a rush of household duties, to stop and pray. With an Englishman's reserve in religious matters, we fear to make ourselves, and even more our sacred office and message, an object of ridicule. On the other hand, much parochial visiting seems to degenerate into mere social gossip and to do no good. 'Am I not wasting my time in mere chat about the weather and the children?' many young clergy ask themselves after a few months' visiting. Now my answer is, Seize every opportunity for prayer, and when in doubt as to whether or not to suggest prayer, *always make the suggestion.* I have never regretted having done so; I have often and often regretted having neglected it. But in this and all things tact must be used, and much will depend on the way things are done. If you find the whole family at tea, or the husband smoking his pipe and the elder boys and girls all hurrying to get ready to go out for the evening, it is clearly best not to suggest prayer. But if you have the mother alone in the afternoon you should certainly pray. I generally say, 'Well, I must be going. But as this is the first time I have called, and as I hope we are going to be good friends, shall we kneel together and ask for God's blessing on the home?' Then I say a short extempore prayer for the home, the children, for a blessing on my visits at all times, that the family may often come out to go into the house of the Lord, and so on. A suitable collect and the Lord's Prayer and Grace close the short prayers. In subsequent visits you need not always pray, though if you don't the women will often say, 'Won't you just make a prayer for me and the children before you go?'—but whenever a suitable opening can be made you should certainly do so. Remember this, working people are much less reserved in religious matters than we are. Also they regard us, rightly and properly, as men of God, and they are much more likely to wonder at our neglecting to offer prayer than at our suggesting that we should do so. And prayer makes pastoral visiting what it ought to be, and prevents it becoming mere social chat and gossip.

Special Visiting

(i) The afternoon house-to-house visiting should lead up to a variety of special visiting, and among such special visiting a first place should be given to the men and lads. It is difficult to make general rules of universal application, but if I were to make any such I should be inclined to say that every parish should have its Lads' Bible Class for boys from the age they go to work to the age—say eighteen years old—when they are fit to join the Men's Class. Many boys simply will not keep on going to Sunday school when once they go to work. Others get broken off through the departure of a favourite teacher, or because of some imaginary affront, or through moving to a new neighbourhood and being too shy to join a strange class uninvited. Never, therefore, visit without asking whether there are any boys of working age in the family who go nowhere. And if there is such a boy, ascertain the best time to catch him, and then call and invite him to the class. I wonder how many of my best and most valued friends I have met for the first time when, as boys of fifteen or sixteen, they emerged from the back kitchen in a shirt and pair of trousers only, mopping their faces with a towel, having been summoned by mother when in the act of 'cleaning' themselves in preparation for going out for the evening. The interview requires tact, and should not be unduly prolonged. Some mothers talk *at* their boys, telling you all their misdeeds, which produces an awkward situation. For the best of mothers are not always wise in this matter. I always ask the boy two questions—firstly, whether he knows any of the boys who already come to the class, mentioning any who live near, and whether he would like one to call for him next Sunday to bring him to class; and, secondly, whether he has any mates who don't go anywhere whom he could bring with him, and whether he would like me to call on them. If a lad has been spending his Sunday afternoons with a friend or two, it is hard for him to leave them. But it is quite simple for them all to come to class together. Often the boy will reply that there is Tom Buckley and Willie Dean whom he goes with, and will offer to show you where they live, so that you may invite them also. This not only gives you a chance of a free and confidential chat in the street, away from indiscreet comments of relatives, but also makes the lad feel bound to keep Buckley and Dean regular in their attendance at class. As I have said elsewhere, a Lads' Club is a great help in dealing with boys, but it is not an absolute necessity, and much may be done without one.

(ii) Besides the boys there are the fathers to be considered in your evening visits. I am inclined to think that the Church of England fails nowhere so generally as in her dealings with the fathers. It certainly is not right that a clergyman should know little or nothing of the fathers of his lads, and the husbands of his faithful women. On the other hand, the women will give you very little help. They are often curiously unwilling that you should visit their husbands. I suppose, poor souls, they fear it will make trouble. I am often told, 'Oh, I would not like you to visit my husband. He's a very funny man. He might insult you.' But you should never give in to this. The only concession I ever make is to say that I won't let them know when I am coming, so that they can honestly say they knew nothing about it. Two of the best women I ever met, both of whom brought up large families of God-fearing children, utterly misunderstood and mishandled their husbands, whom they represented, quite erroneously, as tigers. Naturally the men felt bound to live up to their reputations. And quite recently I had an example of this kind of folly. A woman begged me not to visit her husband, whom she painted as a kind of man-eating tiger. One evening I called in and had a talk with the man when she was out. The tiger sat up and mewed most piteously. Never have I seen a milder beast. 'I've been much to blame, rector,' he said. 'I can't expect our John to stick to his church and grow up good if I don't set him any example. I know it's worried my dear wife a lot. But, please God, we'll alter things in future.' Of course things don't always turn out like this. But a wife's opinion should never be taken as final. Let her tell you, if she will, the best evening and the best hour to catch him, and you do the rest. And with men, unless there are obvious reasons for it, it is best not to press religion too much at first. Make it clear why you have called, namely, to make the acquaintance of the father of a family many of whose members attend your church. I generally add, 'And of course, Mr. Brown, we hope you'll come to us too. It would be a tremendous encouragement to Willie if he had his father coming regularly to the church with him.' But my first object is to get on friendly terms with the man. If he is smoking, I often ask leave to smoke too. Once this involved smoking very bad shag tobacco, for the man always most hospitably pressed his pouch on me. But it was worth it. If you can get a man talking about his work, or hobby, or about politics or sport, you will soon get friendly. Don't agree with every word he says. He won't believe you if you do. But don't be betrayed into an argument. If he asks your opinion, state it clearly, but as a general rule let him do the talking, and let all your attitude be that of a man genuinely interested in social and other questions and anxious to hear both sides. Invite the man to the Men's Class or Men's Service, and don't be discouraged because he does not accept the first invitation. Also seize every opportunity of inviting him personally to any special services in Lent, at the Harvest Thanksgiving, or at special festivals. On the other hand, when you do speak, speak plainly. A man said to me some years ago, 'I don't hold with this church-going. I don't see it does any good.' I replied, 'I don't suppose you do, but that is because you have never given your mind to it. You've never really given yourself to God, and so you've got little good from Him, and He has got no good at all from you. I expect you are the sort of man who has to be red hot to do any good at all. When you've taken as much trouble over your religion for a month as you have over football for the last ten years you'll tell me a different tale.' He took it extremely well, and has since, I hear, developed into a real Christian.

(iii) But boys and men are not the only objects of special visiting. Lapsed communicants should also be looked out for. It is quite extraordinary how many men and women, who have been confirmed, have lapsed from Communion for years. Now it is not the least use to expect that a woman who has not been to Communion for years and years will return next Sunday just because you ask her. It is not to be desired that she should. And equally it is not the least good to suggest somewhere in Holy Week that she should return the following Easter. Some considerable time is required for making up one's mind, and then a good deal of instruction is often needed. Above all, something to supply a special motive for return is necessary. It may be enough that the woman has begun to desire a return to habits of religion, and that she therefore responds to the idea of not being away from Communion at Christmas or Easter. But one of the best possible reasons for return to Communion is the fact that such action on the part of a mother will help and encourage the children. Whether it is a boy or girl who has been confirmed and is getting careless, or one who is going to be confirmed and needs help and moral support, in any case the appeal to the mother is a strong one. So I broach the subject a good way ahead. 'Now Nellie is going to be confirmed, would it not be a good thing, Mrs. Johnson, if you thought about coming back to Communion at Easter? And if you are going to do that you must try to be regular at church on Sunday evenings between now and that time.' If the matter is casually referred to every now and then for a few months the idea becomes familiar. Then it is an excellent thing to hold a kind of preparation class or service of instruction in church for a few weeks before Christmas or Easter, to which such lapsed communicants are specially invited. For many years I held such services at three o'clock on Mondays for three weeks before Christmas and for three weeks before Easter, and never failed to gain a few returned communicants each time. I spent the first two services explaining that Holy Communion is not a spiritual privilege for the few saints, but a help for all who desire it ('He eateth and drinketh with publicans and sinners'); that all Christians ought to be communicants (see rubrics at end of Marriage Service and Service for Churching of Women); and that God is not 'a hard man' who invites us to His table and then is the more angry if we afterwards fall into temptation, but a loving Father Whom we sadly neglect. And many other mistaken reasons for the neglect of Holy Communion can be explained away. Then the last class is used as a devotional preparation.

Similarly, the idea of Confirmation should be put before the unconfirmed men and women you meet in visiting, but put it gradually and with tact. The first time you mention it you may get little response. If, a month or so after, you say, 'And I hope, Mrs. Sullivan, you've been thinking about what I said about being confirmed, now Annie is confirmed and attending so regularly,' you will very likely get a favourable answer. Or the difficulties will be stated. She is 'no scholar,' and is afraid she will look silly in class. Then you can explain that people have to be *instructed* in the Catechism, that is to say, told what it means, but that they do not have to learn it all by heart. And I always explain that many candidates who could neither read nor write have come to my classes, and the other members of the class have never guessed it. Or another woman will say that she fears to look silly going up with a number of little girls. Then you explain that there will be a special 'mothers' class,' and that you have twenty or thirty mothers, or whatever the number is, who will keep her company. In any case, it is quite hard enough for a working man or woman to come forward, and there is no object in making it any harder than it need be.

If in parochial visiting you are constantly on the look out for men or boys for your Bible Class, lapsed communicants to be led back, and candidates for next year's Confirmation, it is wonderful how the work will grow in definiteness, and therefore in interest.

(iv) As you come to know your district well there is a growing danger of over-visiting the sheep and neglecting the goats; of going, that is to say, constantly to that nice Mrs. Smith whose boys are all in the club and choir and her girls in the Guild, and neglecting Mrs. Brown whose children are always irregular, except just before treats. One way in which this may be avoided is by devoting an afternoon a week—or one a month, if this is impossible—to visiting absentees from Sunday school. There are not many teachers who have time for systematic visiting, yet absentees certainly ought to be looked up. They may be ill, and then if not visited you will be told that 'Our Millie lay ill a month, and no one from church came after her.' And, as I have said, the visiting of absentees has this advantage, that it secures your going to just those cases which need it most. Where there is time, the taking out of a monthly, or at least a quarterly, report, as explained in 'How to Deal with Lads' (p. 73), is an excellent way of getting into touch with all parents alike. But few clergy have time to do this for the whole Sunday school. If the clergy are responsible for looking up absentees weekly, it does not seem unreasonable that teachers themselves should be asked to take out the monthly reports. Then you can take the reports out for your own Bible Class.

In addition to visiting absentees, it is not a bad plan with some organisations to visit weak members before the meeting rather than after, on the ground that prevention is better than cure. It is easy during the afternoon's visiting to say, 'You might remind Willie that I am hoping to see him at the preparation class to-night,' or 'Tell Mr. Harris not to forget the C.E.M.S. meeting this evening.' There was a time when I used to fear that people might resent such importunity. On the contrary, they generally seem flattered by it.

Sick Visiting

(i) This important branch of a parson's work must be treated of separately. It includes the visiting of dying cases, of cases of long and serious illness where, however, there is good hope of recovery, and of chronic cases which may last for years. Clearly methods must differ as the case differs. Let us take dying cases first. The most hopeless work with which the clergyman is confronted is the task of visiting people of whom he knows absolutely nothing, and to whom he is not called till the sick person is either unconscious or at the last gasp. I wish to speak with all charity, for in the most dense superstition there is some element of what is good, and in the most superficial observance of the proprieties something to be respected. But it is a sad truth that many people deliberately leave the calling in of a clergyman till the last minute, either because they won't take the trouble to send, or because they don't want the patient 'bothered,' and then run hot foot for a clergyman because it is not considered respectable to let a person die without having 'had a minister to him.' A religious doctor, or district nurse, is a valuable ally, and such will often counsel the calling in of a clergyman. Roman Catholic doctors, to their honour be it said, are specially good in this, even with patients not of their communion. The room will often be found crowded with friends and neighbours indulging in those clamorous expressions of grief and sympathy, and that general orgy of emotion, in which poor women seem to delight. It is better not to interfere with this unless, as too often happens in poor neighbourhoods, many of those present have had too much to drink. In that case I say that I should like a little quiet and, having chosen two of the nearest relations to remain and pray with me, I ask the others to leave the room. Generally they obey without question, but once or twice I have been met with opposition. I never argue. I simply say, 'It is the dying man I am thinking of. I am sure you would not wish to disturb his last hours. Please do as I have said.' Obviously it is impossible to do any pastoral work with a dying man while some half-drunken woman is breaking in every half-minute with panegyrics of the patient's virtues, and with suggestions as to how he should be treated. I am sorry to have to give this caution, but it is unfortunately necessary. Often when the person to whom you are called is thus *in extremis*, you can do nothing but offer prayer. This should never, under any circumstances, be omitted, even if the patient is wholly unconscious, and that for many reasons. Firstly, an obvious reason, we must remember that prayer is addressed to God and not to the person prayed for, and its efficacy does not depend on the patient hearing it. Then, secondly, one can never be certain how much an apparently unconscious man can hear, and familiar words, such as those of the Lord's Prayer, seem to have a special power of rousing semi-conscious patients whom ordinary speech fails to move. And, thirdly, there are always the friends and relations to be considered. Personally, I generally use the Lord's Prayer, a few suitable collects, extemporary prayer based on the prayer in the Office for the Visitation of the Sick, 'for a sick person, when there appeareth small hope of recovery,' and a special prayer for 'those who watch by and tend this Thy servant,' that they may be strengthened and helped, and for all relations and friends that they may be enabled to submit humbly to God's will.

I have said that prayer should always be offered. I do not say that it should always be offered how and when the relatives wish. I had a case quite recently where I was only called in because the district nurse pressed for the presence of a clergyman. The man had been violently opposed to religion, and the wife, herself quite careless, was afraid of a scene. I was therefore sent for at a time when he was likely to be asleep. I knew the circumstances, however, and asked at what times of the day he was usually awake, and said I would return then. When I came back a second time, I was told that he was asleep and could not be disturbed. I said I would wait till he woke up. Up to that point all had been normal, but then the state of affairs became obvious; the woman grew quite abusive, and said that if I couldn't 'make a bit of a prayer and be done with it,' she would send for another clergyman. I said quite quietly that there was no need for that as I was anxious to pray with the patient, but that, as it was his soul I was anxious about, I was sure she would not like neighbours to say she kept a clergyman from him, and so I would stop till he woke up. He awoke in ten minutes, and made no sort of objection to my praying with him, and before he died, which was not till a week or ten days later, he was truly penitent. The truth was the woman feared that there would be trouble, and merely wanted to be able to say that she had 'had a clergyman to him.' If I had yielded I should simply have gratified her respect for the proprieties, and done no good with a man who needed all the help he could get.

(ii) The question is often put as to whether a clergyman should use the Prayer Book Office for the Visitation of the Sick. I have never known one who did, and I am quite convinced myself that it is very unsuitable for present-day circumstances. Fortunately, the rubrics of the office leave the clergyman a wide freedom, and I have found that much of it is useful if freely adapted. As to the direction that 'here shall the sick person be moved to make a special confession of his sins, if he feel his conscience troubled with any weighty matter,' I should like to make a few plain remarks. It appears to me too clear for any dispute that the Church of England offers private confession and 'the benefit of absolution' to all, and forces them on none. Hence it seems to me utterly disloyal to the Church to try and force confession on those who do not desire it, or to make it a condition of admission to Confirmation or Holy Communion. But it seems to me quite as disloyal not to offer it freely to all who desire it. I do not know which is more dangerous to the eternal welfare of a soul, to come to Communion with an uneasy and offended conscience or to stay away for good and all [1] because one cannot quiet one's own conscience. And against either of these dangers the Church provides the remedy of private confession. How any clergyman can reconcile it with his conscience to allow his people to go, as hundreds of thousands of church people do go, in ignorance all their lives of any such help as confession and absolution affords, I cannot understand. I should have thought that there was nothing

[1] I need not say that I am not expressing any opinion as to 'the eternal welfare of a soul' in the case of those who do not receive Holy Communion because, like Quakers and members of some other religious bodies, they do not believe in sacraments. I am writing of those who once received but now stay away because they do not feel fit.

which parochial work made more certain than that many people—especially young people—lapse from Communion because they feel they are not fit and don't know how to get fit. And when they so lapse they are often truly and deeply distressed and in a frame of mind for true repentance. But they are desperate, go off from church and Communion altogether, and grow rapidly hardened and careless. And so it seems to me a plain duty laid on every clergyman of the Church of England to teach his people, and especially those whom he prepares for Confirmation, that they can go to confession, and can 'receive the benefit of absolution . . . to the quieting of their consciences,' if they desire it. Whether they do so or not is clearly no responsibility of the parson. If they don't do so at the time, they will at any rate know about it if the time ever comes when they need it.

Now to say all this is one thing; to say that therefore we ought to speak of confession to every sick person we visit is quite a different matter. For nearly four years I did little else than visit the wards of a big general hospital of which I was chaplain, and both before and after that time I have done a great deal of sick visiting both in and out of hospital, and I have met numbers of cases of dying people to whom a full confession and a sense of reconciliation with God, such as the authoritative pronouncement of absolution affords, would have been of infinite value. But they had never heard of confession, or only heard it described as 'filthy,' 'Roman,' 'unspeakably degrading,' etc., etc. To have spoken of confession in such cases would only have been to have added to the distress of the sufferer, to say nothing of the surprise, suspicion, and indignation of the relations and friends. One could only do one's best, trying for something of the same result under a different name, and solace one's conscience with the reflection that one was not responsible for other men's neglect. But that it is neglect I am deeply convinced. If confession is to be any real help to a dying man, he must have heard of it before the pains of death have come upon him.

Let me close with an example drawn from life. I was called once to a young man of twenty-seven, dying of consumption. His history was simple. At sixteen he got 'broke off,' as they say, from chapel, owing to there being no regular teacher for the youths' Bible Class. From that time he went nowhere, till he contracted consumption. For eighteen months he was home ill, for much of the time confined to bed, but his mother never sent for a clergyman, owing to having had some little bother with the vicar of the parish. At last I was called in. The second time I called I found the young fellow reading his Prayer Book. 'What are you doing?' I asked. 'I'm trying to find out how I can repent for my sins,' he said. 'I know there's something in the Prayer Book about being forgiven, and I want it. I've been bad ever since I was a lad.' I can only say that he was one of the most naturally sweet, gentle, affectionate, and unselfish young fellows I have ever met, and if anyone had got hold of him young he would have made a beautiful character. He, of course, had been brought up at chapel. But are there not church people who try to find out how to repent for their sins, and who know there is something in the Prayer Book about being forgiven, and who desire and deserve plain teaching?

(iii) The second and by far the most satisfactory class of sick cases are those of long illness, either those where from the first there is little or no hope of recovery, or those where recovery is probable. In both cases regular visiting is necessary; in both it is better to go three times a week and stay a quarter of an hour, than daily and stop only a few minutes, and in both cases the thing to be aimed at is to get on terms of the most friendly intimacy. Prayer, unless the person absolutely refuses it, should always be offered. A portion of Scripture should be read, and perhaps also a hymn or a few verses of a religious poem. A gentle stream of monologue will probably be necessary at first, but as you get to know your patient he should be encouraged to talk too. If he admits having been careless, he should be pressed to say definitely how and in what ways he proposes to amend if he recovers. State plainly the obvious truth that God may have laid him on a bed of sickness, not in anger to punish him, but in love to draw him to Himself. Ps. cxvi. and portions of Ps. cxix., especially verses 65–72, may be read. The discussion of how he will amend may lead to an explanation of what his faults have been, whether drinking, gambling, swearing, vice, bad language, or neglect of God. Men are very shy and often hint darkly, and when I first began I often misunderstood them, and either credited them with sins they had not committed or—an even worse mistake—failed to respond to their veiled hints of a desire for advice and counsel. Now, if there is any doubt at all, I go straight to the point. I say, 'My dear brother, if you want my advice and sympathy you must speak plainly, just as you would to a doctor. I am a doctor, a soul doctor, and you need not be ashamed to speak clearly to me.' If then you find a really troubled conscience, confession and absolution can be spoken of.

So far the method is the same with hopeless cases and with those where recovery is looked for. Unless you are asked by the relatives or doctor to break the news that there is no hope, the suggestion that the case is likely to be fatal must never come from you. But it is extraordinary how often people, after long illness, welcome the idea of death. And even when they shrink from it, as is but natural, they can be brought to submit to God's will. Then they will welcome anything you can tell them of the Church's teaching about paradise, the state of the waiting soul, and the life hereafter. And the more they have learned to lean on their Saviour here, the more they will rest in a sense of His personal support and companionship in the valley of the shadow of death. I have found Addison's hymn, 'The Lord my Pasture shall prepare,' useful and much appreciated. There are few happier tasks than that of trying to help and comfort a person who is dying, and knows it, and desires to make earnest and careful preparation.

Where recovery is looked for, careful teaching about prayer, Bible study, and church-going can be given when the sick person is able to bear it, and, as I have said, he should be urged to make some good resolutions as fruit of what he has suffered. And it is a mistake to leave off visiting too soon. Obviously as a sick man or woman gets better, you will have to visit less regularly. But an occasional visit should be paid right up to the time when the patient returns to work, and a little encouragement not to forget what was planned in hours of sickness may be given.

Finally, a hint as to times for visiting may be useful. If patients are found frequently asleep in the afternoon, then time must be found for a morning visit, even at the sacrifice of some reading. But the afternoon is the best time. A very useful time for a short visit in a serious case is 10 P.M. When very busy, I have often said, 'I'll look in to-night, on my way back from the Lads' Club, and have a short prayer for a quiet and peaceful night.' I have always found such visits useful.

(iv) The third class of sick case is the chronic case. Bed-ridden and paralysed people, very old people, and cases of chronic rheumatism. Such people, if they can be interested in the work of the parish or the foreign mission field, may become centres of prayer and spiritual influence. The following rules are useful :

(*α*) Visit each at some fixed interval.

(*β*) Secure for each, if possible, a lady visitor who will visit daily, or at least at very frequent intervals.

(*γ*) If unconfirmed, try to get the patient to desire

Confirmation. Then get the bishop to confirm privately.

(δ) Take the sacrament at regular intervals, say monthly if possible. The lady visitor of each case may be encouraged to communicate with her special invalid.

(ε) In cases where there is a spirit of prayer, make your periodical visit—which cannot be very frequent in the case of chronic cases where the parish is large—the occasion for giving the patient a report of the cases she has prayed for, and a fresh list of cases.

(v) If there is a hospital or workhouse infirmary in your parish, it must be visited, unless there is a special official chaplain. The way in which many large hospitals are left without any chaplain is a scandal, and though it is an undoubted hardship that a busy parish priest, with a large parish to look after, should also have to supply, unpaid and often even unthanked by the hospital authorities, ministrations which take up the full time of one curate, yet the sick must not be neglected. Wards should be visited systematically, names and facts entered in a note-book similar to your street visiting-book, communicants encouraged to receive while in hospital, lapsed communicants urged to return and reported by letter to their parish priest, and the clergy of the parishes near enough to the hospital to make visiting possible may be notified of any cases where a special visit seems desirable. A person's time in hospital is a valuable opportunity.

If there is no hospital or infirmary in your parish, the question will arise, Should you visit your own people when they are in hospital? On the one hand, it seems a pity to spend a whole afternoon, or the best part of it, visiting a case in a hospital where there is already a chaplain. On the other hand, a visit may be extraordinarily fruitful, not only with the actual patient, but with the rest of the household, to whom, of course, you take a report of your visit the same evening. People unapproachable on the subject of religion ordinarily may be quite easily influenced when you go in in the evening and report how 'our Lizzie' or 'our James Willie' looked, and what messages were delivered and sent in return. And, of course, the whole family is invited to kneel with you in prayer for the absent member before you leave the house.

At the risk of seeming to repeat myself, I would say again be sure to kneel in prayer with anyone you visit in hospital. I used to be afraid that by so doing I might seem to be making too much of the illness, or might make the man feel uncomfortable before the whole ward. Both ideas are quite mistaken. There is far more likelihood of the patient thinking you make too little of his sickness than that you make too much. For try and put yourself in his place. Very likely he has never been away from his own home before; he has, after great difficulty, made up his mind to come into hospital; the whole thing to him is a strange, terrible, and unique experience. A man once spoke to me most bitterly of the heartlessness of the nurses—the kindest and most devoted of women—because they laughed and chatted over their tea in the nurses' room, 'with me lying here in the ward ill.' He could not understand that what was so important to him was an everyday incident to them. So you need never be afraid of making too much of a hospital case. My usual formula is: 'As this is the first time I have seen you in hospital, let us offer a prayer for God's blessing on your stay here, that you may soon be restored to your friends'; and then on each subsequent visit I introduce the subject by saying, 'We can make our prayer more of a thanksgiving this time, don't you think?' or 'We had better pray specially for the blessing of sleep,' or some similar opening.

As for making a man feel uncomfortable, I am sure there is no such danger. The majority of working men and women, even if they are not regular attenders at a place of worship, are much more religious than most people think, and if, when you have left the ward, any silly fellow begins making a mock of prayer, the bulk of the men in the ward will fall on him and rend him. Only a few days ago a young clergyman told me that he had followed my advice and prayed with a man in hospital; when next he visited him the man said: 'After you had gone, sir, a clergyman visited the man opposite. But he never said a prayer as you did with me. The other men in the ward remarked on it, and said I had the right kind of parson. I can tell you I felt proud.'

Nursing-homes, orphanages, and institutions of all sorts should also be visited. If tact is used, and you make it plain that there is no desire to 'boss' things or to capture them for the Church, you can do nothing but good. Even when institutions are frankly undenominational you should visit. The staff will be sure to contain some Church members. A nurse once said to me, 'Just because I work in an undenominational institution, the clergy treat me as if I had the plague. I had to take work where I could get it.' So go everywhere where you are welcome, or where you can earn a welcome. Yours is the cure of souls of the whole parish.

General Remarks

(i) When once you have got really to know your parish well, systematic house-to-house visiting becomes at once less necessary and less possible. It is less necessary because that which was undertaken with this very end, namely, getting to know your ground, in view is obviously not so much needed when once the end is gained. And it is less possible because the house-to-house visiting will itself tend, if it has been rightly and fruitfully done, to increase the other types of visiting which demand much of your time and attention. As the people come to know and trust you more, they will be likely to send for you more and more, not only in cases of sickness (though this is and should be your most important and most valuable opportunity for pastoral visitation), but as a trusted friend of the family to advise in matters of difficulty and to help in all sorts of trouble. It may be that you are wanted to 'put together a bit of a letter to our Willie's master' about some trouble the boy has got into, or to help with advice in some legal difficulty, or arbitrate in some dispute between relations after a death, or between neighbours after a quarrel. But whatever may be the causes, and they are innumerable and often not a little comic, it is, as I have said, certain that as you get more and more known and trusted, the calls on your time made by such summonses will grow heavier and heavier, and cut more and more into the time you can devote to visiting of any kind. And so, too, the number of absentees from class, careless church-goers, and lapsed or irregular communicants who need looking up, will increase as the total number of your flock grows. And so regular house-to-house visiting becomes more and more impossible. It may be possible for the clergyman of a small rural or urban parish of 700 to visit every house at least twice a year. I think it should be, though as I have never worked in such a parish my opinion is not of much value. But I am sure it is not possible in a large working-class parish of ten or twelve thousand. But if the parish, or at any rate your special district, has once been thoroughly mastered, renewed house-to-house visiting is of less importance. Nevertheless, every opportunity of going over the whole ground again, even if only in a rapid way, should be seized. If you 'bill the parish,' that is to say, if you leave handbills at each house before Lent, or the Harvest Festival, or the Day School Sermons, or the Dedication Festival—and it is an excellent practice, which might be more widely adopted than it is—I would advise you to take part of your district yourself, leaving the rest to your lay helpers. Thus you can take Henshaw Street, Chatham

Street, and the Model Buildings before Lent, leaving the rest for your helpers. Then the week before the Day School Sermons your helpers can do those streets while you take Salisbury Row, Darwin Street, and Monton Street, leaving Rodney Road, Larcom Street, and Paragon Buildings as your share for the week before the Harvest Festival. Thus you can cover your district rapidly in a year, for mere bill distributing is quick work. In many, indeed in the majority of houses, you will not need to do more than say, 'Good afternoon, Mrs. Walker. I thought I'd call and leave you a list of our Lent services. Put it up somewhere where everyone in the house can see it. I hope they will all try to keep Lent well this year. Are you keeping well? And all the rest? That's right. Well! if I'm to get all my work finished this week I must be getting on. Good-bye.' Such work is not a waste of time, even when no more is done than just to say a few words and leave a bill. The people like it. But more is certain to be done in some houses. You will find new people moved in whom you had not heard about, or old residents who were hostile at some earlier visit become friendly, or some one sick whose illness was never notified, or some other of the thousand-and-one reasons for visiting which would otherwise have escaped notice. I have heard such bill distributing described as 'beneath the dignity of a priest.' I can only say I totally disagree with such a view.

(ii) One final word may be helpful before we leave the subject of visiting. The time may come when, for one reason or another, you have not been doing any regular visiting for a good while. You may have been on your holidays, or ill, or busy doing a colleague's work while he was away or ill, or taken from parochial work by a spell of cemetery or other special duty. Or (for it is as well to be quite frank) you may have got slack, and then your annual retreat, or some other awakening experience, may have made you keen again. How is one to begin visiting in earnest again ? I know nothing more difficult, unless one sets about it in a sensible way. There is the whole parish spread before you, and no particular reason for going to one house rather than another. You might, of course, go and see Mrs. Walker of Brown Street, but there is no object in that more than in going to see Mrs. Jones of Salisbury Row or Mrs. Robinson of George Street. Unless you are careful you will just visit the devout, pleasant, regular church people, who might best be left till last, and neglect just the people who should be visited. And if you do that you will soon drop back into slack ways. I have known plenty of examples of men who were once strenuous parish priests who have in this way insensibly degenerated into dawdlers. And one or two men have frankly owned to me that their reason for seeking a fresh sphere of work, whether a new curacy or a new parish, was that they felt they had grown slack and needed 'a new start in a new field.' But it is not a good thing to leave any place with a feeling of failure you have not attempted to cure. The place in which to overcome slackness is the place where it overcame you. For as 'now is the accepted time,' so I am sure 'here' is the accepted place. What, then, should one do ?

One way is to take out yourself, and deliver by

hand, all the notices of the various classes and guilds [1] for the next month, which are usually sent by post, delivered by lay helpers, or distributed through the school. If one week you deliver personally all the notices of the C.E.M.S., the next week the notices of the monthly class for girls in preparation for Holy Communion, the week after the notices of the similar class for lads, and the last week the monthly Sunday school reports, you will have done a lot of visiting, got into many houses, picked up many dropped threads, and completely restored your former keenness. Since, however, your visiting on these lines will have taken you chiefly, though not of course exclusively, into the houses of the most regular attenders, there is a yet better way. Have a card printed something like this :

ST. JOHN'S CHURCH

'SOMETHING FOR EVERYONE'

For Men.—The Vicar's Men's Class in the Vestry every Sunday at 3 P.M.

For Lads.—Mr. Smith's Class for Lads (14 to 18 years old) in the Church Room every Sunday at 2.30 P.M.

For Girls.—The Senior Girls' Bible Class in the Schools every Sunday at 2.30 P.M.

For Women.—The 'Mothers' Own' Service in Church every Wednesday afternoon at 3 P.M.

For All.—Sunday Evening Service in Church at 6.30 P.M.

[1] See Chapter V, p. 193.

Then get from the day schools the names and addresses of all children who live in the parish. In a big town parish many children are sure to come from other parishes, but your first concern is with your own parish. Go through the lists thus got from the day schools, and note those houses which seem to yield no regular church-goers. All such should be visited. It is easy to say to the woman, 'Of course, Mrs. Jackson, I see your children in day school. But we don't see as much of the rest of the family as we should like to. Can't you find something on this card which would suit some member of your family? See, it has something for everyone. Let me leave you one.' Of course the mere handing in of the card is not much use. You should try and get her to mention some one likely to attend this or that service or class. If you are lucky, she may say: 'I'm sure I wish my husband would go to the class on Sunday. Where we lived before we came to this house, he used to go to the Bible Class,' or 'Our Jim might go to the Lads' Class if there was anyone as would speak to him,' or 'The girls were saying they'd like to take up with school again, but they feel strange going where they don't know anyone.' Then you or the vicar, or the lady who conducts the senior girls' class, can call and clinch matters. As I have said, mere handing in of the cards will effect little, for this shyness of going to a strange class where one is not known is very real and very widespread. But it will go hard with you if the leaving of a few scores or perhaps hundreds of cards does not yield a few new recruits. And at the worst it is a valuable method of renewing keenness on visiting.

One or two critics to whom I have shown the cards have been shocked at my putting the evening service as for all, and at my not putting the Holy Communion at all. I think this is to misunderstand both Christianity and human nature. I do not think it desirable to press the highest duties and privileges of religion on people who are showing no interest in religion at all, and I do not want to invite to Communion lads and girls, or even grown-up people, who are probably quite uninstructed, and who at any rate are making no visible effort to follow up their religion at all. Get them first to instruction and Sunday evening church-going. The rest will follow.

But secondly, human nature being what it is, it does not matter whether you and I want to get such people to Communion, and to attendance at the sung Eucharist or other morning service of Sundays. We shall not succeed in doing so. If you put such invitations before them, they will have absolutely no effect. And perhaps it is just as well that they should not.

CHAPTER III

THE CONDUCT OF SERVICES

Some General Principles: (i) The teaching of the Prayer Book; (ii) The importance of public worship to-day; (iii) Its permanent importance.
The Order of Services: (i) What services ought to be provided; (ii) The value of daily public prayer; (iii) Its practical effect; (iv) Three requisites; (v) Times of service.
The Services in Detail: (i) Mattins and Evensong; (ii) The Litany; (iii) Holy Communion; (iv) Holy Baptism; (v) The Churching of Women; (vi) Holy Matrimony; (vii) Burial of the Dead.

(i) THE Church sets before us, in her Book of Common Prayer, a round of prayer and praise, of feast and of fast, to be observed. Rightly or wrongly—entirely rightly, as I hold—she says that this is the way in which her children are to be taught, trained, and edified. Clearly it is the duty of the Church's officials, her ministers, not merely to provide these services, but to provide them in such a way as shall commend them to the people. I do not wish to suggest for a moment that our Prayer Book is perfect. It was not that when it was first compiled—since everything in this imperfect world is partaker of man's imperfection—and three centuries of growth and change have made it, itself unchanged, less and less adequate for our needs. But to admit that the Prayer Book needs revision is one thing. To act as if the whole principle of that book was wrong is surely another. No one does, and no one I honestly believe can, obey the Prayer Book in every particular, and when men begin branding one another as disloyal, it is usually a case of the pot calling the kettle black. But it does seem to me that there is a duty laid on all clergy to put the Prayer Book into practice *as far as they possibly can.* By all means clamour as loudly and as often as possible for Prayer Book reform. But note two things. First, honest effort will soon convince anyone of the fact that the Prayer Book is much more workable than many people suppose. And secondly, it is to be noted that till the Prayer Book is revised we are in loyalty bound to do all we can to make the best of things as they are. There may be many *details* in which our present Prayer Book might well be amended, but if it is a question of whether liturgical worship is a better thing than the absolute freedom of extemporary prayer and unfettered order, and of whether set forms and days and seasons are valuable, and whether a daily order of public worship is expedient, when, in short, it is a question as to whether dissent was right or wrong in rejecting all the outward framework of the Church's system, then I think the clergy must answer, not in words, but by their actions, in no uncertain tones. One of your first duties is to commend the services of the Church to your people.

(ii) And this is a duty which is of special importance to-day. I am no pessimist, and I am myself deeply convinced that not only are we, as a nation, more sober, more orderly, more moral, and generally more civilised than we were, but that even in purely spiritual things there is improvement. There is, I am certain, more general and sincere interest in religion to-day than there has been perhaps since the days of the Commonwealth. People are dissatisfied with purely material well-being. They have learned, or are learning, that truly 'man doth not live by bread alone.' Much of the silly, shallow, dogmatic materialism of the end of the nineteenth century is dying out. In a word, there is a renewed interest in the spiritual. But this better spirit will come to nothing, producing no lasting fruit, unless it is incarnated in a body of habit and custom. There is no *impression* without *expression*, and unless this greater spiritual aliveness is taught to express itself in a life of worship and devotional exercises, it will come to nothing. The great need of the Church to-day is for worshipping Christians. We want to make the most of the quickened interest in the spiritual side of things to secure praying and worshipping men and women. The real problem of the Church to-day is how to commend her services to religious and spiritually minded men and women. The more the Church at large tries to do this, the more perfectly she will learn what alterations are really needed in the Prayer Book, and how those alterations may best be effected.

(iii) But it is not merely now, under exceptional circumstances, that public worship is a vital necessity. Always, and at all times, it is a necessary part of all true religion. We ought to teach our people that 'the assembling of ourselves together' for holy worship is a duty which we owe to God, to ourselves, and to our neighbours. We owe it to God for His glory only, quite apart from any effect it may have on us. To-day there is a great, and I think growing, sense of duty to one's neighbour, and of each man's responsibility for social wrongs and injustice. And there is a considerable sense of duty to oneself; the duty, that is to say, of developing one's entire nature, body, mind, and spirit, though a man's spiritual development is always likely to be the part most in danger of being neglected. But duty to God seems to be a thing the very idea of which is dying out among us. When I speak to young people to-day of the duty of worship, I am nearly always met with the reply that a day in the fresh air, or time for recreation and study, or necessary rest and relaxation does them more good than church-going. To which my answer is, 'But do you never think of anyone but yourself? If I asked you whether you ever paid any attention or respect to your father, who brought you up and surrounded you with love and kindness when you were a child, would you reply that a cycle ride or a game of golf did you more good than sitting talking to an old man? God is your Father, and you owe Him some attention.' But actions speak more forcibly than words, and one of the first duties of the clergy to-day is to keep the fact of worship prominently before the thoughts and the eyes of the world.

And this, which is a duty to God, is a duty also to our country and our fellow-men. Here and there you may find an exceptionally constituted man or woman who can maintain a vigorous spiritual life without the practice of public worship, but I am sure that this, even if possible for exceptional individuals, is not possible for communities. The nation which surrenders public worship will soon lose all effective religion altogether. Personal and family religion are all important, but they will not long survive, I am sure, the general neglect of corporate public worship.

And though I have admitted that exceptional individuals may be able to develop and sustain a vigorous spiritual life alone and without the help of public worship, I am quite sure that it is not possible for most people. Once again I would quote that fundamental maxim of modern educational theory, that there is no impression without expression. And the most obvious, and in some ways the most fruitful, form of expression for the religious emotions is united public worship. While, therefore, the clergy should be forward to recognise and to welcome religion in those who seldom or never come to church, they should do everything in their power to promote church-going. Very silly people often say that the clergy think nothing matters but going to church, and not very wise clergy often seem afraid of incurring the taunt. Personally, I never make any concealment about my aims and objects. I am a parson, and proud of it, and one of my chief objects is to get people to church. And the man, woman, or child whom I cannot get to attend church is a man, woman, or child with whom, to that extent at any rate, I have failed. Let us admit that, in individual cases, some who don't go to church are better than others who do. But either our whole profession is a mistake —which I don't believe, or I should long ago have sought another one—or church-going is a thing to be worked for. Numbers, we are frequently told, are not everything. I can only say I never heard anyone use that absurd phrase of anything he really cared about. From the politician seeking votes, or the tradesman customers, down to the cricketer seeking runs or the schoolboy postage-stamps, everyone recognises that numbers do matter. Your duty is to fill, or at least to try and fill, your church, and to that end you should strive to commend your services.

The Order of Services

(i) The first question is what services we ought to provide. I have no wish to be dogmatic on a subject upon which better men and better scholars than myself differ from me, but I confess that the minimum which seems to me compatible with loyalty to the Prayer Book is daily morning and evening prayer, and a celebration of Holy Communion on every Sunday and holy day. I open my Prayer Book and find myself faced by the words: *The Order for Morning and Evening Prayer daily to be said and used throughout the year.* And I read that 'all Priests and Deacons are to say daily the Morning and Evening Prayer either privately or openly, not being let by sickness or some other urgent cause,' and I cannot believe that the urgent cause contemplated by the Prayer Book is the sort that will recur six mornings and five evenings a week throughout the year. And the further direction about ringing a bell to summon people to pray with the minister, seems to me to make the mind of the Church quite clear. And the first post-Communion rubric, in which there is no provision about being let by any cause whatever, seems to me equally clear in respect of Sunday and holy day celebrations of Holy Communion. I would therefore, in all affectionate earnestness and charity, urge my younger brethren to ask themselves very seriously whether this minimum of services is not incumbent on them.

(ii) The value of daily services is obvious. Prayer has a value in itself, and if the enclosed orders of the Roman Church, which devote themselves solely to prayer, represent an ideal which is probably beyond what man can attain to—for surely all prayer and no work must be as fruitless in most cases and as difficult to maintain as all work and no prayer—they are at least glorious witnesses to the claims of prayer. And so a service is of value though none but the angels are present to pray with the minister. Then, again, daily prayer and frequent celebrations afford a great and priceless help to the clergy in their busy lives. If we allow the daily office to be one more duty to be got through, rushing in at the last moment and rushing off again to the urgent engagement, it will merely be one more care and worry. If we study to be quiet and to do this, our own special business, with loving care and attention, the daily services become little islands of rest and peace amid the distractions of the day's work, and supply a true rest cure to troubled nerves. But, above all, the daily services are valuable for the people's sake, affording them opportunities of prayer and praise when they can avail themselves of them, and continually keeping before their minds the great fact that the clergy are, or should be, first of all men of prayer, ministers of Christ, and stewards of the mysteries of God. I say that this is above all the value of daily prayer, for the clergy may, and of course must, offer up prayer for themselves and their people privately whether they have public prayer daily or not. And if the daily offices are not said publicly, the priest's own private devotions may be his rest cure. But nothing but the daily services and regular ministration of the sacraments will supply the people with the opportunities they need, nor will anything else so surely establish the true idea of God's ministers in the minds of the people. Many years ago I was curate in a parish where there was not merely daily morning and evening prayer, but also a daily midday service. One day an old army pensioner, who lived near the church, said to me, 'If all church bells went three times a day to call folk to prayer there'd be no talk of disestablishment. That bell going like that day after day is the true Church defence.'

(iii) But the recitation of the daily offices in church, and the provision of frequent celebrations, has a practical value. Such a daily order of Church life supplies, as it were, a groundwork on which it is easy to build. What I mean is this. If there are daily services to which a few people are accustomed to come, it is easy on special occasions to add special weekday services to which many people will come. But if the church is seldom used, if indeed it is shut from Sunday to Sunday except for a Wednesday or Thursday evening service, then it is very difficult to get people to come to church at all on weekdays. I have noticed again and again that, on occasions of intercession or thanksgiving, the special services in even well-worked parishes have been poorly attended if the daily offices are not usually said, and well attended if they are the rule. The daily offices keep things going, if I may so express myself, when there is nothing special on.

(iv) If daily offices are said publicly there are three requisites, and they are:

(*a*) Regularity.
(*β*) Punctuality.
(*γ*) Reverence.

(*a*) Regularity is the first. It is not the least use expecting people to come to church for daily services if they see those services omitted, or the hours altered, for any and every cause, to suit the parson's convenience. This is specially the case with the weekday celebrations of Holy Communion. I wonder how many times I have myself, when on a holiday or when staying for a night in a strange town, taken the trouble in the evening of looking at the notice-board of some church to find a suitable celebration, only to find the church closed the next day. Once I took a twenty-minutes' walk for an eight o'clock celebration, only to find the caretaker just locking up. 'Oh, it was at seven this morning,' he said. 'The vicar had to go away for the day, and he told the only lady who ever comes.' Another time I got a courteous note from the vicar, regretting my disappointment, but explaining that notice had been given in church the week before that the usual services would not be held. But if occasion arises when the usual services announced on the church notice-board *cannot* be held, a large and clearly printed notice to that effect should be pasted on the notice-board itself. But everything possible should be done to avoid alterations. I know of one church where the hours of the daily Eucharist have not been altered or the service omitted since the church was built, more than a quarter of a century ago, and several others where the same is true of the time since the daily Eucharist was started. The order of the celebrations, daily or weekly, should be as immovable as the course of the sun.

I would not say quite as much of the daily morning and evening prayer. But this I am sure of. It is regularity that tells. There was an old man, whom I knew, who was much moved by the impassioned complaints of the clergyman at the neglect of daily services by the laity. He said to his wife: 'After all, I'm vicar's warden, and I'm getting an old man, and I don't need to get to the office as early as I used to do. If I went to Mattins it would only mean missing my half-hour in the garden after breakfast. I think I'll tell the vicar on Sunday that he can count on my being at Mattins in future whenever I am not ill.' Next Sunday the vicar gave out that as he would be taking his holidays for the next four

Sundays there would be no daily services or Thursday celebrations for the next five weeks. My old friend decided that if weekday services could be so lightly suspended they could not be of any very great importance, and returned to his garden. I know the difficulties in parishes where the clergy are single-handed and a *locum tenens* bargains for Sunday duty only. But if daily services really matter, it is surely better to pay extra for a *locum tenens* who will take them.

And there is another point worth mentioning. Where there are two or more priests on the staff, the times of services should, if possible, be such that all can be present at all services except on each man's day off. In a parish where there are a number of clergy, if none are present except when 'on duty,' as they say, it inevitably produces the impression that they only go when they are obliged. And then the laity only go when they are obliged, which is never. And there is another thing. Many lay people, even educated people and regular church-goers, are shy of making the responses when they are by themselves in the congregation. Only the other day a highly educated lady said to me: 'I always avoid Saturday mornings, there are generally so few present then, and I really don't know what I should do if I were the only person present. Indeed, I have often peeped in to see if there was anyone in church before I came in.' If there is a clergyman to lead the responses as well as to take the service, this difficulty would not be met with. It may seem that I am setting too high an ideal. But surely the staff of a parish should be a kind of college of priests, who would naturally seek to say their daily offices all together.

(β) Punctuality is quite as necessary as regularity. If you have to be at business at 9 A.M. it makes a great difference whether the service begins at 7.30, as announced, or at 7.40 or 7.45. A small church which I used to attend as a layman had a daily celebration at 7.30 A.M. The last time I visited it the new priest-in-charge began the service at eleven minutes to eight one day, and at nine minutes to eight the next. On each occasion I was the only person present; which did not in the least surprise me. I have never been again, and I never mean to. And I could name more than one other church where fine weekday congregations have been scattered by unpunctual clergy. One especially had the finest weekday services I ever knew. But the congregation was rapidly reduced to two old ladies by a vicar who was always late.

Clergy sometimes allege as an excuse, 'Our people are very unpunctual. It is impossible to begin on the stroke.' But that is the very reason for beginning on the very stroke. Nothing tends to produce punctuality in the people like punctuality in the priest. The best way of ensuring punctuality is to purchase a good vestry clock, and then take care to be in the vestry at least a quarter of an hour before celebrations of Holy Communion, or services where for any reason there is much to prepare, and at least a clear five minutes before the daily offices.

(γ) The third requisite is reverence. The services

of the Church should be said much more slowly than is usually the case, and the clergy should take much greater pains about distinctness and audibility. Nothing annoys the laity so much, and there is nothing about which there are such frequent complaints, as the muttering and gabbling of the service by the clergy. What many of the clergy forget, is that constant practice has enabled their tongues to fashion words and their ears to catch sounds much more rapidly than is the case with even educated laity, while as for the less educated people, they often do not catch one word in twenty. There is a passage in Stevenson's book, 'The Wrecker,' describing the signing on of sailors for a voyage, which I should like to make every candidate for Holy Orders learn by heart. It runs:

'A long and wordy paper of precautions, a fo'c's'le bill of rights, must be read separately to each man. I had now the benefit of hearing it five times in brisk succession; and you would suppose I was acquainted with its contents. But the Commissioner (worthy man) spends his days in doing little else; and when we bear in mind the parallel case of the irreverent curate, we need not be surprised that he took the passage *tempo prestissimo*, in one roulade of gabble—that I, with the trained attention of an educated man, could gather but a fraction of its import—and the sailors nothing.'

Frequent repetition makes it easy for the clergyman to take the service too fast; and it is a danger to be carefully guarded against. Only a few weeks ago I had a letter from a thoroughly intelligent girl, a day-school teacher, in which she said, 'They take the daily services here at such a breakneck pace I can't understand a word. I can't even join in the Creed. I think I shall leave off going on weekdays.' And as I have said, such complaints are of frequent occurrence. On the other hand, I have only twice in all my life heard complaints of a clergyman being too slow, and in both cases it was really unpunctuality in beginning, and unnecessarily long pauses during the service rather than slow articulation that was complained of. Some little time ago I and a devout working man, a great C.E.M.S. worker, were at a weekday service taken by two clergy, and I struggled between amusement and pain at the way in which he tried to say 'We beseech Thee to hear us, good Lord,' while the clergyman who was making the responses to the other clergyman's reading of the Litany said something that sounded like 'Seechee t'hear us goo-lor.' I would therefore urge on my brethren the importance of reading slowly, giving each syllable its full value, paying due attention to commas, and in every way trying to make the service easily understood and truly appreciated by the people. Let them try also for a pleasant, natural, unforced delivery. All mannerisms, all affectations, all unnatural roaring, gabbling, or droning should be guarded against. I am quite sure that anything, whether in reading the prayers, or in reading the lessons, or in preaching, which can be recognised as distinctively 'clerical' is wrong. Your aim should be to deliver what you have to say or to read so as best to convey what is said or read to your hearers. It is a good thing to watch others, both so as to avoid their faults and to copy—to a limited extent—their virtues. But the great thing is to be audible and natural. Don't resent criticism. The grumpy church officer who tells you that no one can hear you at the back of the church, that you speak too fast, that you hang your head down so that the sound does not travel beyond the first few pews, that you clip your words, and drop your voice at the end of a sentence, etc., etc., is a much truer and more valuable friend than the gushing lady who tells you she *did* so enjoy your *lovely* sermon last Sunday, and *does* so hope you will let her know *whenever* you are preaching. Indeed, it is not a bad thing to ask some sensible friend, who won't gush, to tell you plainly when you speak too fast, or are inaudible, or commit any other fault.

Finally, never rest till by constant practice you can read the service and lessons as perfectly as possible. And when you think you are perfect, try and improve. Regarded simply as literature many of the collects of the Prayer Book are masterpieces, fit to rank with the noblest passages of Shakespeare. And an actor who delivered Hamlet's soliloquy as the collects are too often delivered would be hooted off the stage. Nothing will do more to bring the laity to church than distinct, reverent, and intelligent reading.

I have sometimes been told by young clergy that they hate 'preaching the service.' If by preaching it they mean delivering it in an affected, unnatural, and professional voice, they are doubtless right. But if they can so deliver each service that it may have the effect of a sermon, why should a man whose life's work is the preaching of the Gospel of Christ be sorry that he has an opportunity of making each service a true preaching. Woe is me if I preach not the Gospel.

(v) One other point remains to be dealt with before we pass on to consider the services in detail. It is the question of the hours of service. If we want our people to make use of the services of the Church, especially the daily services, we must choose those hours which are most suitable to the people. Mattins at 10 A.M. in a working-class parish is a mere derision. And many parishes, where the clergy complain that no one comes to the weekday celebrations of Holy Communion at 8 A.M., would gather good congregations if the service were put at 7.30 A.M. or 7 A.M. It is really surprising that the clergy don't think of these things. I know one large working-class parish where the vicar and curate say Evensong daily at 5.30 P.M.; a time nicely calculated to be too early for all who go to work, and too late for all who don't. Obviously, no one could be expected to attend at such an hour, and the daily tolling of the bell merely advertises to the laity that the Church's services are not for them. In the morning an early hour is always to be preferred to a late one. I have known clergy, at parochial missions, to declare that no one in the parish was likely to come to a 5 A.M. Communion, and then to find the church half full at that hour. At any rate, a person who goes to business at 8 o'clock *may* come to church at 6.30 or 7 A.M.; he certainly can't come at 8 or 8.30. And it is our duty to provide opportunities. And while speaking of opportunities, there is one further thing that needs saying. A daily celebration is one thing ; what are called frequent celebrations are something quite different. If my birthday, or the anniversary of my Confirmation, my marriage, or my mother's death, occurs on Tuesday, there is an obvious motive for going to church on that day. There is no earthly reason for going the following Thursday rather than on the previous or the following Sunday. And so I have known several parishes where occasional weekday celebrations were poorly attended, but where a daily one was always well used.

The same is true of extra celebrations at an early hour on Sunday. Suppose you have, in addition to the weekly celebration at 8 A.M. on Sundays, one at 7 A.M. on the first Sunday in the month, for servants and hospital nurses and busy mothers. Some will mistake the Sunday, especially if there are five Sundays in a month. Others will forget. Anyone who oversleeps himself will not have another chance of communicating for a month. A hospital nurse may be on night duty, or specially busy for some reason or other, on just that Sunday. So the numbers dwindle till the question is raised, 'Whether it is really worth while keeping on the seven o'clock celebration in view of the poor response.' If it had been weekly, the numbers would probably have grown instead of declining.

My point is this : if there is really any demand for a service at a particular hour, there is a demand for it every week. I do not want to seem to advocate the needless multiplication of services.

The Services in Detail

(i) Mattins and Evensong, the daily offices of the Church, call for consideration first. After many years of trial, I do not hesitate to say that an early hour for Mattins, before breakfast rather than after, is a blessing to a clergyman. It gets him up, and it enables him to get into his study for work at nine instead of somewhere about eleven. One curate whom I knew kicked rather at daily Mattins at 7 A.M. when it was first suggested. After some years of it, he declared that nothing would make him return to Mattins at ten o'clock. In most parishes, especially if there is a daily celebration, the clergy will probably say Mattins alone or with only a devout few. If it is placed before the celebration of Holy Communion—liturgically its proper place—it will help to secure that the latter service begins punctually.

Evensong, however, should be so placed that an appeal may be made to the laity. In well-to-do parishes the afternoon, in working-class parishes the evening, will be the natural time. But every parish has its own special needs. Much may be done to popularise Evensong, if the expression may be allowed. If the clergyman can play, or if a player can be depended on, a small harmonium may be placed in a convenient place and the canticles be sung, and a hymn used at the Third Collect. Or, in addition to the mid-weekly sermon on Wednesday or Thursday, one night a week may be used for special intercessions.

For many years I have followed the following plan on Mondays. First a notice is printed in the magazine, as follows :

MONDAYS IN AUGUST.

2nd. Bank Holiday. No intercessions.
9th. For the parish.
16th. For the Church at home.
23rd. For the Church abroad.
30th. For special needs.

Then at Evensong the canticles are sung and the service taken to the end of the Third Collect. The order after that is :

Hymn ; short address (delivered walking up and down in the aisle) ; Lesser Litany and Lord's Prayer ; three collects (introduced by 'Let us pray that God would hear our intercessions and prayers,' and then the Collect for the Tenth Sunday after Trinity ; 'Let us pray for the guidance of His Holy Spirit,' and the Collect for the Nineteenth Sunday after Trinity ; 'Let us pray for Foreign Missions,' and a suitable missionary collect) ; simple petitions, to which the people reply, 'We beseech Thee to hear us, good Lord' ; a second hymn ; St. Chrysostom and the Grace.

I have found this form sufficiently elastic to meet all needs, and the people have responded always and in all places most wonderfully. The address, which should not be more than seven or eight minutes, may deal with the special subjects to be prayed for, or with general principles of prayer. For the special needs, the people should be invited to send in requests for prayer.

On saints' days or their eves a hymn and a five minutes' address will be welcome. People talk about the needless multiplication of sermons. But a set sermon is not required. A few simple thoughts simply expressed to direct the prayers and touch the hearts of the people is all that is necessary. And certainly people do come to church more readily when there is an address. Where there is unwillingness to come to weekday services it sometimes springs from uncertainty as to how long those services will last. In putting out notices of services, it is not a bad thing to print at the foot of the paper: 'Persons attending these services may count on getting out of church at —— o'clock.' And then keep rigidly to the time named, regarding even a minute over as a breach of faith. When once people get accustomed to coming to church on weekdays, they will come readily to plain Evensong when there is neither hymn nor sermon. In these days of rush and hurry prayer is a true rest cure, and in poor parishes, where homes are small and crowded and noisy, many people are thankful for the quiet and beauty of the church and for half an hour with God.

(ii) The Litany will in many parishes be best said at Mattins on Wednesday and Friday. But in parishes where there are people able to come to church during the morning, it can profitably be made a separate service. Only one thing is imperative: it should never be said under circumstances which render it necessary to hurry it. It is one of the most beautiful of human compositions, and the glory of the Church of England. Even Mr. Blatchford has felt its spell and used extracts from it as a preface to one of his works. Yet it is regarded by many people as dull and wearisome. This is due to the way in which it is rendered. Personally, I much prefer *said* to *sung* Litany, but even when singing it the priest need not divest it of all expression and meaning. If a short address, preceded and followed by a hymn, is inserted just before the Prayer of St. Chrysostom, the whole makes a service of about half an hour, very suitable for a Wednesday or Friday morning in Lent or Advent, or indeed the year round.

(iii) The Holy Communion is, of course, the chief service of the Church, and the way in which all classes of parishioners, male and female, young and old, use it or neglect it may be taken as a fair indication of the success or failure of the clergyman's work. As to the best hours for Sunday and weekday celebrations I shall hope to speak later. I will now confine myself to hints for the guidance of the celebrant himself.

First let me point out that all that has been said about unpunctuality, irregularity, muttering, and gabbling, and all other forms of carelessness and slovenliness apply to the clergyman's attitude towards the Holy Communion more strongly than to any other part of his work. There is no service where any lack of care and effort will be so fatal alike to the priest and his people.

A man just ordained priest should get an experienced clergyman—his vicar for choice—to take him carefully through the service. So long as there are various 'schools of thought' in the Church, it is useless to expect any uniform standard of celebrating. But that is no reason why every man should be a law unto himself. And when any man has chosen his methods he should, if I may be allowed the expression, standardise his movements and gestures, so that the same movement may always accompany the same words. Such matters as the position of the hands, when a book is not held, are important. An actor knows and appreciates the importance of the right use of the hands and arms. Nothing produces a worse effect than to see the priest drift up anyhow to the altar, and when there stand anyhow in any ungraceful attitude. Mr. Kipling, in his barrack-room ballad 'The 'Eathen,' implies with no little truth that much of the effectiveness of the British soldier comes from learning to put his socks straight and 'lay 'is mattress square.' Similarly, few men realise, till they have tried it, how much orderly and disciplined movement makes for reverence and beauty. So too the young priest, while never hesitating to use a book when necessary, should try to learn the commandments, invitation, absolution, comfortable words, and other portions of the service said facing west, by heart, so as to be able to say them without a book. Only while you want a book take the big one from the altar, and hold it firmly in both hands. Nothing looks worse than to see the priest surreptitiously consulting a small prayer-book held in one hand. Indeed, it is a good thing to learn as much of the service by heart as possible, since there is nothing which so helps one to make each word of it one's own. A really great pianist once told me that he could never put himself and his own feelings into a piece of music till he had learnt it by heart; then he could make it truly his own, the expression of his own emotions. And I have always found that the same is true of prayers said by heart, as contrasted with those merely read.

All notices should be carefully and legibly written out beforehand, so that they can be delivered clearly and intelligibly. It is a good thing to adopt a regular order, thus: (i) Celebrations of Holy Communion for the following week and Sunday; (ii) other services for the week in chronological order; (iii) meetings, other than public services, in church, in the mission, and in school; (iv) extra-parochial meetings; (v) other notices. This order makes it easier for the congregation to understand and remember the notices than it is when there is a long stream of notices in which services in church and public meetings in the town hall, and mothers' meetings in the vicarage, and Church Lads' Brigade parades in the parish hall are all jumbled up together.

The same applies to lists of subjects for which the congregation is asked to pray. These too should be carefully prepared beforehand. I do not think we make nearly enough of this way of teaching our people to pray. Not merely should the names of the sick, the dying, and the departed[1] be read out,

[1] In places where the bishop of the diocese, or anyone else, objects to requests for prayer 'for the repose of the soul of A. B.,' no objection will generally be made to the phrase: 'You are asked to remember before the throne of God the soul of A. B., entered into rest.'

but requests for prayer of all sorts should be encouraged. In one parish, where there was a 9.30 A.M. celebration weekly for working-class mothers, intercessions were always read out, such as the following: 'You are asked to pray for a husband out of work, for a son and a daughter out of work, for a son who has taken to gambling, for a woman who is drinking, for a soldier son in India, and for a family sailing for Canada next Wednesday.' The district visitors used to collect requests for prayer during the week, and mothers valued the opportunity so much that they often said: 'If you'll please to have our Ernest prayed for on Monday, I'll make a push and try to come.' We need in all troubles and difficulties to take what worries us and 'spread it before the Lord' (2 Kings xix. 14).

Finally, let me beg of all my brethren to have nothing to do with altar cards, or manuals which interpolate portions of the Roman order of the Mass into the Prayer Book service. Either our Anglican service is adequate or it is not. If any man thinks it is not, the sooner he leaves our communion and joins one where he will find what he believes to be necessary, the better. If it is adequate, it is surely unnecessary to pad it with needless additions and repetitions. To say this is not to say that our English rite is perfect, or that it might not profitably be enriched by proper authority. But for each clergyman to add to it as he thinks fit, or for unauthorised people to do so as if with authority, is surely intolerable. Each man, when celebrating, will naturally use his own private prayers. And there can be no harm, and indeed must be much good, in men studying other liturgies with a view to seeing what direction those private prayers may best take. But my own experience—and my early training was all in the opposite direction and led me to use for years all the interpolations given in 'Notes on Ceremonial'—makes me believe that the fewer additions the better, and that no one realises the beauty of the English rite till he uses it *just as it stands*.

(iv) The sacrament of Holy Baptism has been sadly and strangely neglected by those who, under the influence of the Oxford Movement, have done so much for greater dignity and reverence in the celebrating of the other great sacrament. And thereby a great missionary opportunity is lost. Every opportunity should be taken to make the administration of Holy Baptism as impressive as possible. There is no justification for neglecting the clear directions of the Prayer Book and having it half an hour before a weekday Evensong instead of 'after the Second Lesson' as ordered. I fear it is impossible to administer it only on Sundays and holy days, since the majority of English people don't know what holy days are, and would never remember to bring children for baptism on a holy day. But whatever evening in the week is selected for the administration—and it had better not be the night of the midweekly sermon—Evensong should be said, and a few of the faithful should be urged to attend and make a congregation.

Baptisms should be taken after the second lesson, and the service can close at the Third Collect with the prayer of St. Chrysostom and the Grace. This will not keep the relations and friends unduly long, and should help and impress them. On Sundays it may be necessary to take baptisms apart from any other service—though occasionally they may very profitably be taken at a children's service—but from time to time a baptism at the ordinary Sunday Evensong is a great object-lesson to the whole congregation. Where the position of the font makes it impossible for the majority of the congregation to see the ceremony a temporary font may be placed just in front of the chancel, in the position usually occupied by the litany desk. The service should be rendered as impressively as possible, and it should be made clear that baptism at Sunday Evensong is a privilege reserved for (*a*) the children of regular communicant members of the church, and (*b*) for cases where all the sponsors are also communicants. After such a service many people will remark on the impression it has made on them.

With regard to the presence of godparents, I feel very strongly. Many clergy tell me that they cannot bring themselves to 'turn away a little lamb from the fold' because its parents bring no sponsors. I do not think there is any need to turn away a child. When a child is refused for lack of godparents, the address should always be taken, and the case visited to secure the child's being baptised later. But I very much question whether the clergy have any right to give the Church's privileges except on those terms on which the Church offers them. As for the people who can't find anyone to stand for their children,

I simply don't believe in their existence. Such excuses spring from mere carelessness, laziness, and indifference. I have known cases where women have sent their babies to be christened in the charge of a neighbour's child of twelve, and when remonstrated with have said, 'Oh, well, I never bother, and I thought it would amuse the little lass to take it.' This sort of thing, combined with the slovenly way in which baptism is administered in too many churches, is responsible for much of the neglect of religion so common to-day. Whether children brought without godparents are to be refused, is a point which the vicar and not the assistant curate must decide. But I can bear witness that in the two parishes in which I myself enforced the rule, the number of baptisms in a year rose as compared with the number before the rule was made binding. In parishes where the vicar refuses to allow children without sponsors to be sent away, the curate might form a band or guild of sponsors. Only let it be a big one, and let the members recognise an obligation to try and look after their godchildren. For one pious woman to stand for a couple of hundred children a year for ten or fifteen years running is to make the whole thing a farce. It is extraordinary that religious people should be willing to take such solemn promises so lightly on their lips.

Before the service interview the sponsors and get the children's names written down. This obviates many difficulties. Sometimes it is impossible to understand what the parents say, and a long dialogue, in the middle of the service, between a puzzled clergyman and a flurried and nervous woman is not a thing that tends to reverence. Only a week or two ago it took me nearly five minutes in the vestry to discover that what sounded like 'Siranly' was really Sarah Ann Leigh. Also poor women, when asked to 'name this child,' will often give the surname as well. If you then say, 'But you don't want it christened Ellen Wilkins, do you?' they will say, 'Yes, sir, Wilkins,' and then explain afterwards that that is the father's name. Again, a talk before service gives you a chance of persuading parents not to handicap their children with absurd names. Why should an unhappy boy go through the world called Ladas, after the Derby winner of 1894, or Jubilee John, or Mafeking, or Adam Abel Cain? A little friendly advice goes a long way. I doubt if, where the proper number of sponsors are provided, one has any right to refuse a parishioner. Fortunately, the only time when I positively refused to accept a name, when a man who had had some drink wanted to have a boy christened Jubilee Bouncing Boy, the parents lived in another parish. The mother only consented because she was afraid her 'master would be awkward if anyone crossed him, as he had had a little drink.' When the man was sober the boy was christened Stanley, and the man thanked me for not having allowed him to make a fool of himself. Finally, a word with the sponsors before the service is specially useful when children of some age are brought. Often a mother, bringing a baby, will bring also a sturdy child of three or four who has been neglected, owing to illness or some other trouble when it was a baby.

But it is no pleasant job baptising a kicking and screaming boy of four who shouts, as I heard a sturdy Leeds child shout: 'Nay! ah we'ant. Nay! ah do'ant like him. Mother do'ant let him. Ah we'ant.' If you talk to the child beforehand and make friends with him, all goes quite quietly.

Have a baptism shell, and a napkin to wipe the child's forehead with after the pouring of the water. Learn how to take the child, so that it sits, as it were, on your left hand and lies along your left arm, with the head resting in the curve of your elbow. Take the service slowly and impressively, trying to make every word carry its full meaning to people who perhaps seldom go to church. I do not think there is any harm in substituting a short extempore address at the close of the service for the address to the god-parents which is given. The similar homily at the end of the marriage service is only to be used 'when there is no sermon,' and so by analogy a sermon may surely be substituted here for the address given.

Adult baptisms should, of course, be taken on a different night to infant baptisms. Everything possible should be done to make the most of so great an opportunity. Notice must be sent to the bishop at least a week before. The service should be taken at the proper place, after the second lesson, on a saint's day eve, Whitsun Day eve for preference. The proportion of unbaptised adults is terribly high in many parts of England. No candidate should be presented for Confirmation without the strictest inquiry as to baptism.

(v) The Churching of Women should not be

taken only when Holy Baptism is administered. Opportunities for it should be afforded before or after any service. Many women will not go anywhere or do anything till they have been churched, and it is a great hardship if they have to wait several days for an opportunity. And I have known women who would not allow an unchurched woman across their doorstep. The woman to be churched should kneel at the altar rail. At this, and indeed at all services, if she is bareheaded, she should be told to put her shawl over her head. The service to the end of the psalm should be said facing the woman. From there on the priest should face east. At the close of the service I always say, when holding the alms-bag to the woman, 'There is no need for you to make any offering, but you may do so if you wish.' They always give if they can afford it, and there should be no idea of *payment*. I also say, if the churching is before a service, 'You need not stop for the service now, unless you wish.' Many women are not strong enough for a long service, yet don't like to walk out of church unless told that they may. On the other hand, it is well to encourage your communicant mothers to be churched before a celebration of Holy Communion, and to receive the sacrament afterwards.

(vi) Holy matrimony is a subject which must be treated in some detail. Whereas it is only very seldom that a man will deliberately attempt to behave irreverently at a baptism service, as in the case quoted in paragraph (iv), it is unfortunately true that bad behaviour at weddings is terribly common.

The bridegroom is often nervous, and attempts to pass it off with horse-play; or a middle-aged woman in the company, with a local reputation as a wit, thinks it incumbent on her to play the fool; or the whole party have been drinking, and one or two have taken a good deal too much. I have seen many weddings which were deplorable exhibitions of levity and profanity. The clergy can stop this if they choose, and they ought to do so. No matter how large or how ill-behaved a crowd there may be, a clergyman can always get quiet and order if he chooses. The other day I had to marry a young rough who, though not drunk enough to be sent away,[1] had had a good deal to drink. He deliberately guyed the service, to the giggling delight of the bride and the whole party. I let it go on for a few minutes, and then said, 'My lad, you're neither so silly nor so ignorant as you pretend. You've come here for a very solemn service, not to play the fool. If I speak to you again, I shall ask the whole party to sit down for half an hour to think where you are and what you are doing.' There was a short battle of looks, but he quickly subsided and behaved like a lamb. When they left the church, I told the verger that I expected he would beat his wife before nightfall. I don't know if he did, but he had run away and left her in less than ten days. Personally, I wish that universal civil marriages were the rule, so that the Church might

[1] No clergyman has any right to marry a man or woman who is not sober enough to know what is happening. No lawyer allows a man to sign his will when he does not know what he is doing. Yet a will can be revoked next day, while marriage is binding for life.

take no hand in such marriages, but might reserve her blessing for her own children. But while the Church has to marry all sorts of people, the clergy should insist on reverence. If a marriage seems likely to be rowdy, I go into church before the service and request all women without hats either to cover their heads with shawls or to leave the church. This has a sobering effect. I then add, 'We are met here for a very solemn service, and those who do not mean to join in prayer for the bride and bridegroom can at least behave with reverence. I shall be glad to have silence in the house of God both before and during the service.'

Let us now take the service in detail. The rubrics are so scanty and so puzzling to the laity that the priest should tell the parties what to do. You should have the names of bridegroom and bride—say John Arthur and Elizabeth Ann—written on a piece of paper and placed in the Prayer Book. Go in and kneel for a moment before the altar in prayer. This is not merely right as a preparation for so solemn a rite, but has the further advantage of letting the people see that the service is a religious one. Then stand at the chancel step and let the verger place the wedding party, the man opposite your left hand, the woman opposite your right. Whoever is to give away the bride should stand behind her. The best man stands beside the bridegroom, and one bridesmaid beside the bride. Say to the man in a low voice, *Is your name John Arthur?* and to the bride, *Is your name Elizabeth Ann?* This not only ensures your having the right names, but prevents your marrying the best man or a bridesmaid by mistake. Then say to the bride, if necessary, *Take off both gloves, please. You can give them and your bouquet to your bridesmaid to hold for the present.* Then read the two prefaces, the first loudly, for all the congregation —who should remain seated through all the first part of the service—and the second one, which begins *I require and charge you both*, more quietly, as addressed to the bridal couple only. When the questions have been asked and answered, say, *Who giveth this Woman to be married to this Man?* adding in a low tone to the person acting as father of the bride, *Give her right hand to me.* Then turning to the bridegroom you say, *Take her right hand in your right hand and say after me:*

'I John Arthur—take thee Elizabeth Ann—to my wedded wife—to have and to hold—from this day forward—for better for worse—for richer for poorer—in sickness and in health—to love and to cherish—till death us do part—according to God's holy ordinance—and thereto—I plight thee my troth.'

When the groom has said this after you, sentence by sentence, you say *Separate hands*, and to the bride, *Now take his hand again, the same hands, and say after me.* The woman repeats the words after you in the same way. Then say, *Put the ring on the book.* You may say silently a short benediction over the ring. Then say in a low tone to the man, *Take her left hand in your left hand, and taking the ring from me* (here give him the ring), *and putting it on her finger* (here touch her finger, the one next the little finger, to show him which one to put it on), *say after me :*

'With this ring—I thee wed,—with my body—I thee worship,—and with all my worldly goods—I thee endow :—In the Name of the Father,—and of the Son,—and of the Holy Ghost.—Amen.'

Then say, *Let the bride and bridegroom alone kneel on the chancel steps ; the rest of the bridal party remaining standing.*[1] *Let us pray.*

After the prayer, say in a low tone to the groom, *Remain kneeling, but take her right hand in your right hand.* Then lay your own right hand on their joined hands, and say clearly for the whole congregation to hear :

'Those whom God hath joined together let no man put asunder.'

After the announcement to the people, and the blessing of the kneeling couple, you bid the married pair rise. Say quietly to the bride, if necessary, *Take your gloves and bouquet again. You can put on your gloves if you like.* Then add, a little louder, to the rest, *Let the whole bridal party follow me to the altar.* Then walk slowly before them to the altar saying the Bridal Psalm. On reaching the altar, the psalm being ended, the bridal party should be arranged at the rail, the women kneeling on the left

[1] The advantages of this are twofold : first, it makes it clear that the blessing is pronounced on the bridal couple and not on the whole party ; secondly, a single mat on the chancel steps is all that is required, and there is no need to strew the aisle with kneelers over which everyone will trip at every opportunity.

of the bride—towards your right—and the men on the right of the bridegroom. Then say loudly enough for all to hear, *Let us pray*. Here all the congregation should kneel. If books or cards are handed to the bridal party, they should be given to all except the married couple, for the responses are made *for* but not *by* them. At the close of the service I tell them all to stand, and address the married pair as follows, in place of the printed address:

At the close of the service it is always the privilege of the minister who has taken the ceremony to offer a few words of advice and council to those who are newly married. I want to remind you of one of the three reasons for which we said, at the beginning of the service, that matrimony was ordained. It was ordained, we read, for 'the mutual society, help, and comfort that the one ought to have of the other, both in prosperity and adversity.' Now I can well believe that you mean to be a help and comfort to one another in your married life. But I want to remind you that you should be a help and comfort to one another not only in those times of joy and happiness which we hope are before you, and in those times of trial and of trouble which come to all of us in this world, but also in that which is the true end and object of our life here, the service of God. No home can be blessed where God is forgotten and His service neglected. And there are three chief ways of serving God—namely, daily prayer, the study of His Holy Word, and worship of Him in His house. It is an excellent thing, when hours of business and other duties allow of it, for husband and wife to say their prayers together. Where this is impossible, at any rate let the husband know that his wife prays morning and evening, and let the wife know the same of her husband. Then, too, let the Bible be an open book in your home, a book often read and studied. If I know and love my Bible to-day it is because my mother taught me to read it aloud to her as a tiny boy, and because my father loved to hear his children read it. Above all, as to-day you have come to church for God's blessing on your married life, so come out week by week to worship Him in His holy house. Let no Lord's Day pass without a visit to the Lord's house. And then if God hears our prayer and grants you the greatest of all earthly blessings, the blessing of children, they will grow up good, because they will see their parents setting them an example. And be sure that we, in this place, will not fail to pray that God may bless your married life abundantly.

I then say to the bridegroom, *Give your arm to your wife, and let the whole bridal party follow me to the vestry.*

When any of your regular members, especially communicants, are married, it is well to make as much as possible of the ceremony. I fear the time for the revival of the Marriage Eucharist is not yet. But often a devout couple will make their Communion together early on the day of the wedding. A couple of hymns at the marriage service itself will be much appreciated. In that case the bridegroom and his party should be in church, sitting in the front rows near the chancel, before the bride arrives. She and her party should be met by the clergyman at the door, and should come up the aisle on her father's arm, followed by the bridesmaids and the rest of their friends. The clergyman, having given out the hymn from the church door, should precede the bridal procession slowly up the aisle as the hymn is sung. If a familiar tune is used, there is no absolute need for a choir. The second hymn should be sung as the bridal party go from the chancel to the altar, the psalm being sung afterwards when they are standing at the altar rail. It is wonderful how people appreciate any effort on the part of the clergy to add dignity and beauty to a wedding, and I have known cases where, at no expense, and at no greater trouble than the provision of a lady organist to play two hymns and 'The Wedding March,' the service has been declared to be 'So beautiful; such a privilege.' The desire for a little pomp and ceremony at a wedding is a perfectly natural and legitimate one, and it should be the clergyman's pleasure to gratify it.

(vii) *The burial of the dead* affords to the wise parish priest a great opportunity. The directions in Dr. Dearmer's 'Parson's Handbook' are no doubt well suited to country churches with their own churchyards, but impossible for most town parishes where interment is in some distant cemetery. But a black altar frontal, however cheap and plain, should be obtained, and the desire for a special requiem celebration on the morning of the funeral encouraged. I have known more than one case where active Protestant objectors, aggrieved parishioners, have said, after such a service for one of their own relatives, 'Well, I'd never say a word against that. It was just what we all felt we wanted.' Then the body should be brought into church for the first part of the funeral service, only the committal and the Grace being taken at the grave-side. Where there are sure to be many strangers unused to church ways, the simplest and best-known hymns should be used. Personally, I always use 'Jesu, Lover of my Soul,' which is sung after the Lesson. If the amateur organist can play 'The Dead March,' or 'Oh rest in the Lord,' or even any quiet hymn tune as the procession leaves church, it produces a good effect. I always go up to the cemetery quickly in a tram, so as to be ready to meet the funeral at the cemetery gates and precede the bier to the grave-side. Even an entire afternoon is not wasted if it does something to touch a family at a time when any impression is easy and may well be lasting.

I know that in some parishes there is a rule that none but communicants, or the children of communicants, are allowed to be brought into church. I understand the feelings which prompt this rule, but I don't share them. Such a rule seems to me to act unfairly. Must one refuse to a large family of devout Sunday school teachers and altar-servers permission to bring into church the body of a loved—and perhaps quite justly loved—father because he was not confirmed, while a whole family who never came near church can have every privilege when they bury the one confirmed member? Personally, I think the church should be open to all baptised persons who do not die by their own hands. Of course with anyone who has lived in open sin, and whose life has caused a scandal, it is different. But in that case a quiet word to the friends, pointing out the unfitness of making any special parade of the religious ceremony, is generally enough.

CHAPTER IV

THE MINISTRY OF THE WORD

Some General Considerations: (i) Its importance; (ii) Its difficulties.
The Sermon: (i) Its manner; (ii) Its form; (iii) Its matter.
Choice of Subjects: (i) Gathering topics; (ii) Keeping a note-book.
Some Practical Suggestions: (i) Method of preparation; (ii) The value of practice.
Alternatives to Sermons: (i) The exposition of a passage of Holy Scripture; (ii) Lectures; (iii) Demonstrations.
A Few General Considerations: (i) The dignity of the pulpit; (ii) Preaching to special classes.

Preaching

(i) THERE is no subject which has to be treated in these lectures which I approach with greater keenness or greater interest than that of preaching. It should be every clergyman's aim to make himself, not certainly a great preacher, God forbid, but the most effective preacher possible. It is one of his supreme duties. He is called to the ministry of the Word as well as of the sacraments, and woe to him if he preach not the Gospel. I hope that the silly habit of decrying preaching, which was common among the junior clergy twenty or five-and-twenty years ago, is dying out. Preaching is the only way of arousing people to understand and desire the sacraments, and the only way of securing a right and fruitful use of them when the desire has been aroused. Preaching is always necessary in every stage of one's people's spiritual development, to convert, to instruct, to edify, to encourage. And along with pastoral visitation it is the one sure and unfailing way of filling a church. A man need not be learned, brilliant, eloquent, or original; if he is in earnest and is careful in his preparation, he will always secure hearers—yes, and grateful and attached hearers.

(ii) Its object being, as has just been said, to convert, to instruct, to edify, and to encourage, the methods adopted by the preacher must obviously vary with the object aimed at. And when with these various objects we consider the variety of people addressed—young and old, devout and careless, educated and simple, rich and poor—and the variety of circumstances under which sermons have to be preached—in big and stately churches and in homely mission rooms, out of doors, in schools and gaols and hospitals, at home and abroad—it is obvious that one single style of preaching will not do. How often I have seen clergy fail because their style, excellent in its way, was quite unsuited to the particular occasion. A man stands up in a mill yard during the dinner-hour and, in a thoroughly clerical voice, preaches a scholarly and closely reasoned sermon of the firstly, secondly, thirdly type, and wonders that the men only a few paces away continue smoking, talking, and reading their papers, and the boys and girls scatter to their games. Or in some important church, crowded with instructed church people, a clergyman stands up in the middle of a stately and dignified service and preaches a short slangy address, or one where the first elements of religion are explained with needless detail and illustrated with childish stories, as if the congregation were children or heathen. These are, of course, extreme cases. But how often we have all heard, at the end of a quiet day, the remark, 'Very interesting and thoughtful of course, but I should have liked more time for silent prayer. It was more suited for a Sunday evening sermon'; or at a Harvest Thanksgiving, 'Very beautiful of course, and would have done nicely for our devout people on Wednesday morning, but I fear it hardly touched the crowds.' The cure for all these mistakes is to be natural and preach as you would talk. Eloquence, fine language, moving power, these things will come. But the first thing to be aimed at is to acquire a natural unforced style, and the power to say what you want to say in such a way that the people before you will understand your message. The art of preaching is, of course, distinct from, but nevertheless allied to, the art of writing. And the only way to become a successful writer has been declared to be to have something to say, and to say it. As a man gains mastery over his stores of matter and over his own powers, he will naturally develop along the lines that suit him best. But at first a plain and unadorned simplicity, and a constant effort to attain the obvious end of preaching, namely, the conveyance of one's meaning to one's hearers, are the surest way to proficiency.

The Sermon

(i) When we come to consider the question of the sermon itself, the first point to be decided is the manner of its delivery; should it be written or delivered *extempore*? Or, rather, since this division of sermons into written and extemporary scarcely corresponds with the actual facts, let us rather ask whether a sermon should be read, delivered from memory more or less exactly as written, delivered from pretty full notes, or delivered entirely without notes, or at most from the barest headings. I do not think it is either possible or desirable to lay down a general rule on this point for everyone. But there are one or two considerations worth remembering. First of all, there are circumstances in which a written sermon to be read to the congregation word for word from manuscript is clearly out of the question. Such are, for instance, preaching in the open air, in hospital and workhouse wards, and similar occasions. Or a man may find himself suddenly called on in an emergency when the expected preacher has failed to turn up. A man wholly dependent on his manuscript will find himself sadly at a loss under such circumstances. Or a man may find himself in a position similar to one in which I found myself as a deacon, when I went to preach in a Lent week night in one of the school missions in South London. The church was a subterranean cellar, there was neither pulpit nor preaching-desk, and the only light was a dim gas-light immediately behind the preacher's head. The only alternative was to turn one's back on the congregation and preach with one's manuscript to one's nose and one's nose in the gas-light, or to discard manuscript and preach without it. And since that trying evening I have often met difficulties almost as great.

Secondly, there are plenty of circumstances where, though it is quite possible to preach from manuscript, it is not, I think, desirable. Thus, when speaking to children, it is almost impossible to keep their attention without looking at them while speaking. At a mission, too, it is necessary to be guided very largely by the impulse of the moment, to discard much that has been prepared, to follow up some suggested line of teaching or exhortation, and generally to be as little tied and as completely spontaneous as possible. A close dependence on manuscript is here a very real hindrance. Again, at devotional services and prayer and intercession meetings it is often helpful to walk up and down the centre aisle. Clearly here manuscript is out of the question. And there are many other occasions when a sermon wholly read is out of place.

Thirdly, it is undoubtedly true that the vast majority of people, at any rate among the working classes, greatly prefer an extempore sermon. Within the last few days a very regular church-goer said to me: 'I couldn't seem to enjoy his sermon. He read every word, and never raised his eyes from his book. It was good when you could listen to it, but

I can't keep my attention when the preacher reads it all.'

These considerations might seem to decide the question in favour of extemporary preaching. But there is much to be said on the opposite side. No one capable of judging would, I suppose, deny that Dr. Liddon and Mr. Spurgeon were two of the finest preachers of the past generation. And each of them both wrote and read every word, I believe. And without wishing to say that Canon J. G. Simpson of St. Paul's is the best preacher in the Church to-day —for comparisons are odious, and there are many fine preachers I have never heard—I certainly have never heard a finer, and he both writes and reads every word. Now it is not possible, of course, to found a general conclusion on a few examples. But my own belief is that no man reaches and gains the first rank as a preacher who does not systematically write his sermons. And I am sure if men wrote their sermons out in full more oftener than they do, the general level of preaching in the Church would be greatly improved. Lack of form, poverty of matter, extravagance of language, diffuseness, undue length and inability to come to an appropriate end, are all faults which lie in wait for the extemporary preacher.

I should therefore be inclined to say that the ideal sermon method, certainly for the first ten years of a man's ministry, and for all his life if his characteristics require it, is that of writing the sermon in full and then preaching it from notes. The notes may be full or slight, they may be used in the pulpit or left in the vestry. But they should be made. I myself had done a great deal of speaking at debates, both at school and at the Cambridge Union, and had preached for more than three years at an almshouse in Cambridge, and had also done some political and other public speaking before I was ordained. Yet my first vicar insisted on my writing my sermons, and I am sure he was right. I wish I could now find time to write more often and more fully than I do.

(ii) The mention of notes leads us naturally to our second point. After the manner of preaching, extemporary or from manuscript, the question of the form of a sermon must be considered. Many sermons, I fear, might be described as being without form and void. Every church-goer who is accustomed to follow the sermon carefully will have noticed cases where what was evidently meant to be a brief introduction has swelled till it has taken up most of the allotted time; or again, cases where what was meant to be a side issue, introduced perhaps merely as an illustration, has grown so as to destroy the whole proportion of the sermon. This is often the case when a man writes a sermon. Even experienced writers know what it is to set out to write on some topic and to have their pens run away with them, so that they write something quite different from what they intended. But this which happens easily when a man writes, happens yet more easily and often when one is speaking. Whether, therefore, you are going to write a sermon, or to prepare one to be delivered from notes, begin by drawing up a skeleton or scheme. A man who has been writing leading articles for the last dozen years for a great daily paper, told me the other day that he never wrote anything without first drawing up a scheme. 'If I do,' he said, 'I find that what should fill three-quarters of a column has spread to a column and a quarter, or that I've developed three unimportant points and omitted the one that really matters.' No doubt he exaggerated, speaking in jest, but the extraordinarily clear and beautiful prose he writes is probably due in part to his habit of writing to scale.

An illustration may be useful. Take the text 'For to me to live is Christ, and to die is gain' (Phil. i. 21). We might draw up such a scheme as the following:

Introduction.—The Apostle in prison; unable to do the one thing, namely, preach the Gospel, his heart is set upon; his enemies are everywhere active; reports of faults and of failures reach him from all his fields of work; he whose one boast it has been that he will preach without pay, and that none shall say he lived by preaching the Gospel, has become a pensioner on the bounty of the Philippians. Yet this epistle is marked by its tone of sunny cheerfulness and love. This is the sort of religion we want. What is its secret? Our text—

A. '*For to me to live is Christ.*' (i) *Christ the plan.*—So many lives without plan. So many plans, some better, some worse. To follow Christ the best plan.

(ii) *Christ the power.*—It is one thing to map out a plan, another thing to realise it. 'I can do all things through Christ, who strengtheneth me' (Phil. iv. 13).

(iii) *Christ the prize.*—The best laid plans may fail. We may miss the prize. It may prove worthless. Christ alone never fails.

B. '*To die is gain.*' (i) *Death part of the plan.*—In every other plan death comes as 'the dread Fury with the abhorred shears.' But if it is Christ's will, it is part of the plan.

(ii) *Death the final victory.*—See Collect for Easter Day. Cf. also 1 Cor. xv. 26 and 55.

(iii) *Death is the gaining of the prize.*—Cf. Phil. i. 23.

Conclusion.—This, then, is the sort of religion we want. This kind of faith has power in our own lives and those of others (1 John v. 4 and 5).

I have not given this example because of any special value or originality of the ideas, but because it illustrates what I mean by 'form' in a sermon. Students of music will recognise its resemblance to sonata form, with its introduction, statement of first subject, statement of second subject, development and coda. But as not all musical compositions need be sonatas, so not all sermons need fall into this form. A single subject treated under heads, firstly, secondly, and thirdly, is easier and often quite as effective. Or, to stick to analogies from musical form, a man who has gained, by practice and diligence, full control over his matter and manner, may on some occasions dispense with form and indulge in what a musician would call 'variations on a theme.' What I mean is, he may take a single idea, such as the thought of God's love for us, or His untiring providence, or the attraction of Christ's

Person, or some other central thought, and view it now from this side, now from that, turning it and embroidering it, so to speak, with quotations from Holy Scripture, from the poets, and from noble literature, and illustrating it with examples from life and literature and, in a word, letting the central thought lead him where it will. This type of sermon is very suitable for brief fifteen-minute addresses at devotional meetings or on weekday evenings. But while this type of address seems far easier than the more formal sermon, it is really far harder, and can easily degenerate into a mere formless talk, in which the preacher seems to say first one thing and then another, with no particular reason for saying them and no connection between them when said. A really good sermon of the 'variations' type should be like a string of pearls, each thought separate, beautiful in itself, and joined with all the others by an unseen string.

An alternative to drawing up a sketch and writing to it may be found in first writing the sermon and then analysing it carefully. But this appears to me very distinctly the less helpful way as, if the sermon has got out of hand in the writing and become lop-sided, it will be a difficult and tedious matter to bring it into shape again. But whether written to a sketch, or written first and then analysed, a good sermon should analyse well. The more shapely a sermon is, the easier it will be for the preacher to deliver and for the congregation to follow and to remember. Dr. Boyd Carpenter, in some ways the most remarkable extemporary preacher I have ever heard, and a master of beautiful and many coloured language, told me, when he was Bishop of Ripon, that he often arranged his points for a sermon like the squares of a chess-board, and that then, having a clear mental picture of the board before his eye, he could proceed leisurely from square to square or, if the sermon seemed likely to be too long, could miss a few squares, or a whole line or lines, picking up the thread of his discourse at any point, without allowing the break to be noticed. I have often listened to him since, and can well believe that this was his method. But few men have his gifts, his command of language, power of pictorial imagery, and marvellous memory. But some such plan might suit many preachers after considerable practice.

While we are considering the art of preaching, especially while we are thinking of the form in which the sermon should be cast, and the way in which the effects aimed at may be obtained, there is one piece of advice I would give, though it is so obvious that it seems hardly to need mention. I mean advice to the beginner to study the works and methods of the great masters of the art. In every other work the beginner who desires to excel knows that he must put himself to school, as it were, with the masters of his craft, trying to see how they get their effects, striving to improve his own technique by a study of their methods. What the young painter, sculptor or musician, the young surgeon or barrister does, the young preacher should do also. Try when possible to hear great preachers, not merely for the spiritual help you may gain from them, but also (and I am sure there is nothing wrong, but rather much that is praiseworthy in such a course) that you may *learn how they do it.* Only take care to hear different types of preachers, with different manners and methods, and avoid founding your own preaching on the model of any great preacher. I have known one or two men who have become mere copies of this or that famous preacher, and even when there is no conscious lack of sincerity or reality, and there is always the danger of such a lack, a poor copy of a great preacher is a wretched thing. I do not want you to copy great preachers; I want you to learn by a careful study of their methods.

This may be done by those who, either from pressure of work, or because of the place where they live, have little chance of hearing many great preachers, by reading and analysing books of printed and published sermons. There are few more helpful things for a young preacher than to read a sermon, by some fine preacher, carefully and then make a full analysis of it. I once was in the vestry when a really great preacher had been preaching. The vicar of the church, who had heard the preacher many hundreds of times, having formerly been his curate, said to him, 'To-day was the first time that I have ever managed to detect the framework of a sermon of yours. I have often wondered how you did it. You seem just to stand up and talk, without notes and without plan, and yet everything comes out in the right order. I knew you must have a plan, but usually the skeleton, which gives shape to the whole thing, is so perfectly clothed in flesh that one never suspects that it is there. But to-day I could see the ground-plan. I could almost have named your firstly, secondly, and thirdly.' Now what easily escapes us in listening to a spoken sermon should be clearly enough seen in analysing a printed one. And it is really extraordinarily interesting to strip the flesh from a sermon by a real master and see the underlying skeleton which gives shape and coherence to the whole. It is more than interesting, it is instructive. And you need not be, indeed you should not be, above taking hints about other things besides the mere form or skeleton of the sermon. Notice how he gets his effects; what use he makes of quotations, whether from the Bible or general literature; how he uses poetry; and perhaps above all, how he manages his peroration and closes his sermon, so that the end seems neither sudden nor long drawn out. Why should a preacher be the only artist who scorns to study the fundamental principles of his art? Why should a clergyman not learn his business as other business men do? It is true, of course, that the best sermon is the one in which God most completely speaks *through* you. But as the spirit of a man can express itself best through a well-trained and disciplined body (the greatest musical genius does not think he can become a good pianist unless his fingers are made, by constant practice, readily responsive to the mind), so the Spirit of God speaks most freely through a well-trained and disciplined mind.

I need scarcely say that the object of reading and analysing other men's sermons is not that you may use them as your own, any more than the reason a young painter copies the cartoons of Raphael is that he may publish the copies as original paintings. You do your studying and analysing to learn. I do not say that you should never preach another man's sermon. In a time of great pressure of work you may be forced to do so, and to preach another man's sermon is certainly better than to go in utterly unprepared and waste your time, and that of the congregation, with mere vapid talk. Though even so, unless you are prepared to take a volume of printed sermons into the pulpit and read from it, the labour necessary to assimilate another man's sermon and make it sufficiently your own for effective delivery may well be as great as that needed for writing one of your own.

Neither do I say that it is necessarily dishonest to preach another man's sermon without acknowledgment. I know some clergy say that if you are preaching a borrowed sermon you should begin with some such introduction as, 'Pressure of work having prevented my preparing a suitable sermon, I propose to-day to give you one by Dr. Liddon,' or whoever it may be. This is a point for each man's conscience. I have known many good men who would have thought it needlessly scrupulous and affected to do so. But if you do borrow anything more than a hint or suggestion, be careful how you borrow. In this, as in all relations of life, a little common sense is a good thing. I once heard a clergyman I knew well deliver Newman's famous sermon on Heb. xii. 14 (the first in vol. i. of 'Parochial and Plain Sermons') to an educated congregation as if it were his own. After the service I went into the vestry and said, 'Do you know what you've done? You have just delivered the most famous sermon in English pulpit literature as if it were your own.' 'Oh! have I,' he replied quite undisturbed. 'I heard it on my holidays and it seemed rather good, so I just took a few notes.' He might just as well have delivered Hamlet's soliloquy as his own original composition. But if you read to learn, and to enrich your general store, you can't read and digest too many sermons. Newman, Keble, Liddon, Phillips Brooks, Walsham How, and the great living masters. And don't neglect Spurgeon and that master of exegesis, the late Dr. McLaren of Manchester. And while you read make notes on the margin. I know many book-lovers regard this as a barbarous practice. But a book which is being used, so to speak, as a lesson-book may rightly be treated a little differently from other books. And after a few years it is very interesting to re-read a volume so annotated. I have just been re-reading some sermons of Newman's, so read and analysed years ago, and find one marked 'Read at Cambridge: re-read at Poplar, April 1898.' Such details have an interest and even a value.

(iii) I have written at considerable length about the form of the sermon, because the best matter, if presented, as is too often the case, in a formless, ill-arranged, and unsuitable way, is of little help or value to anyone. I know many devout, thoughtful, and educated men of whom people say, 'There's always something valuable in what he says if you can keep your attention fixed. But he's so difficult to follow. It's such an effort to listen to him.' Such men are wasting much of their energy, and effecting for their Master much less than they might have done if they had from the first striven to acquire a good manner of writing and delivering their message. Yet such men are, I am sure, far more valuable to the Church than many men whose fluency, showy language, and attractive manner conceal an almost total absence of solid thought. There are men who prompt one to ask, at the end of half an hour's fire-works, 'What has he said?' and of whom one is forced to reply sadly, 'Nothing at all.' But if you have ever put this question to yourself about another man's sermon, it can do you no harm to put it to yourself frequently about your own. When you have finished writing a sermon, and are reading it through in your study, ask yourself, 'Why was this sermon written?' If you can find no better answer than 'To occupy a twenty minutes' interval between two hymns next Sunday morning or evening,' put it in the wastepaper-basket and try to write another which does at any rate aim at something. We all miss our aim at times. But what if we have no aim?

It may help us to attain definiteness in our aim if we recognise that all sermons are addressed to the Intellect, the Will, or the Affections, or to two, or to all three, of these faculties. We might classify sermons roughly as those addressed:

To the Intellect: (*a*) Doctrinal; (*b*) practical; (*c*) expository; (*d*) historical.

To the Will: (*a*) For conversion; (*b*) for reproof

and correction; (*c*) as exhortation to some definite action.

To the Affections: (*a*) To induce love of God or man; (*b*) penitence; (*c*) faith in God's providence; (*d*) interest in spiritual things.

I do not say that any sermon can, or perhaps ought to, fall exclusively into any one class. A sermon in which the preacher tries to give his people the Church's teaching on some great religious truth, and which may therefore rightly be classed as a doctrinal sermon, will effect little unless there is some appeal to the will—some effort, that is to say, to get people to accept the doctrine, and some appeal to the affections, an effort that is to stir and warm their hearts towards God, Who is the source of all truth. And the sermon which has as its supreme end the conversion of sinners will profitably rest on an exposition of some passage of Holy Scripture, and be driven home to the hearts of the hearers by some efforts to awaken penitence, and so will be addressed to the intellect and affections as well as the will. But I cannot doubt that it will be a real help to distinguish, if only in our own minds, the instructive, the hortatory, and the emotional types of sermons and the different classes of each. For one thing, it will prevent our falling into a stereotyped manner of preaching. A young friend of mine said to me some time ago, of the clergyman whose church he attended, and whom he was really fond of: 'I get so tired of his sermons. When you've heard one you've heard all. There's no variety. Even when they are about different things they seem the same.' I knew well what he meant. And then, again, it is obvious that the manner of a sermon must vary with its object. Not only will a mission sermon, aiming at conversion, differ in its language and manner of delivery from an instruction on Church doctrine or a devotional address on the love of God, but one type of instruction, say on the Church's teaching about Confirmation, will differ much in manner and method from another, say on how to pray. And so with other types of addresses.

But it is not enough to have an aim. We should have one suitable for our people. I remember once asking a really clever young University don to address a large class of very rough lads. He had seen them in the club, and he knew something of the conditions of their lives. Yet he gave them a long, closely reasoned, and extremely able defence of theism. He might as well have addressed them in Greek. Better, indeed, for they would have admired his powers. As it was, they merely thought him dull. It is therefore not enough to have an aim in writing a sermon. One should have an aim suitable to the special congregation which is to be addressed. In this we shall be helped by that intimate and personal knowledge of our people which visiting alone will give. This leads me to my next topic.

Choice of Subjects

(i) On sitting down to write a sermon the first point to be settled is, What shall I preach about? And here we have many helps. Does the season of the year suggest one? If Advent or Lent is near, would a sermon on the best way of observing those seasons be helpful? Obviously it is better to preach on such a subject a few Sundays before the special season has begun, so as to give one's people time to think and make their plans, rather than on the first Sunday of the season itself. Or, again, are the summer holidays near, and would it be well to speak to one's people of the duty of observing their religion while away from home, and of the great opportunity of doing something for the service of God which a fortnight in a boarding-house presents? Who knows what might be effected by the example of a family, or of two young men, or even of a single person, getting up to go to Holy Communion, or keeping Sunday carefully, in a seaside boarding-house? Or if the season suggests nothing, does the work of the church or parish suggest a topic? Has the attendance of Communion been poor? Have you been pained when visiting to notice the prevalence of bad language? Does the number of unbaptised children you have met with suggest a sermon on the doctrine of Holy Baptism, and upon 'this charitable act' of bringing children to this sacrament? Have conversations you have had with people while visiting suggested any difficulties upon which your people would be glad for instruction? Has a devout Sunday school teacher asked you to preach on some difficult passage of Holy Scripture, or has some one, in a letter signed or anonymous, asked you to deal with the question 'Why does God allow wicked people to go unpunished?' or 'Why do the best people often suffer most pain and trouble?' or some similar topic?

Sermons called out by circumstances like these (and there is no reason why you should not mention the special reasons why a particular topic has been chosen) will be more vivid and lifelike, and will be felt to be more helpful and interesting, than sermons which seem to have no special reason for having ever been written. And the habit of preaching special sermons for special reasons will produce the desired occasions. People who have heard other folk's difficulties discussed and cleared away will submit their own to you. Parishioners who find that you welcome serious questions when visiting will be encouraged to open their minds freely when you call. There will be something like competition among the Sunday school teachers, church officers, and others, in submitting interesting matters for treatment. But it cannot be expected that you should be always provided in this way with subjects ready to your hand. You must make provision beforehand.

(ii) If a clergyman wishes to be never at a loss for a subject, he should keep a notebook and jot down subjects for sermons as they occur to him. Everyone must have noticed, I suppose, the way in which some text in the daily psalms or lessons, heard maybe a hundred times before, will one day strike on one's ear with special meaning. Then is the time to book the text with a few brief notes of the thoughts suggested. I will give a few examples of what I mean. I was once going to do a very difficult piece of work, which I regretted having undertaken and which I feared would be made more difficult by dissension among those engaged in it. The evening

from my own experience, of the way in which verses of psalm, or lesson, or gospel which we have heard a thousand times will suddenly seem to glow with new meaning and helpfulness. When this occurs the verse should at once be entered in one's notebook. But it is not enough to book the text; some brief notes of the thoughts suggested must also be jotted down, or it may well happen that you may be asking yourself in bewilderment some weeks after, 'Why ever did I make a note of that text? What ideas did it suggest?'

Along with such texts as strike you in this manner, note also in your notebook any of striking nature, whether for the beauty of the language or for any other quality. Nothing so attracts one's people's attention, and disposes them to listen, as a text which sets them thinking, 'Now what will he say about that? Why did he choose it?' I myself when I was quite a small boy heard a sermon on the words:

'The pots . . . were of bright brass. In the plain of Jordan did the king cast them, in the clay ground between Succoth and Zarthan' (1 Kings vii. 45 and 46).

The preacher's idea was that the stiff, cold, sour clay which was useless for agriculture, yielding neither corn nor wine, was just the place for casting the bright vessels for the service of God. So times of trial, sorrow, sickness, bereavement, and trouble which yield nothing of worldly prosperity (corn) or happiness (wine of life) are well suited for preparing bright vessels for the sanctuary, shining instruments for God's service. The working out was beautifully done, but it was the text that made it stick in my memory. And five-and-twenty years afterwards, when I had been a clergyman for some years, I met a lady who had heard the sermon and remembered it.

Again, I heard two clergymen, neither of them three years in orders, preach on the two texts: 'Give me a blessing; for thou hast given me a south land; give me also springs of water' (Joshua xv. 19); and 'None saith Where is God my Maker, who giveth songs in the night' (Job xxxv. 10). I do not mention these examples because I want my readers to make use of them, and still less because I think a preacher should always be seeking unusual or startling texts. But I do think originality in this, as in other matters, has its value, and if, when you are reading the Bible, a text strikes you forcibly, you should make a note of it, since if it strikes you it may well strike others too.

But the Bible is far from being the only book which should yield subjects for sermons and suggestions for your notebook. Obviously your theological reading, whether doctrinal or historical, should suggest single sermons and courses. So should what I have called your own subject, no matter how remote it may seem from theology. Mr. Houston Chamberlain's 'Foundations of the Nineteenth Century,' a very queer and unequal book, much overpraised before the war and very unjustly decried since war was declared, supplied me with half a dozen courses of sermons.

Novels too, if really good, are always suggestive. One of the most beautiful Christmas sermons I ever heard, preached from the text, 'A little child shall lead them,' opened with a brief but well-done résumé of Bert Harte's 'The Luck of Roaring Camp.' All Mr. Anthony Hope's novels seem to me full of insight into character and accurate psychological analysis, and I should not like to say how many sermons I have owed to his novels, especially 'The King's Mirror,' 'Double Harness,' 'The God in the Car,' 'Quisanté,' and 'Second String.' But I recognise that every man has his own tastes in fiction. But any good novel, worthy of the name, should increase your knowledge of human nature and of the springs of human action, and so enrich your preaching. Nor need you be ashamed to quote from good novels in the pulpit.

But much as you may learn from books you should learn more from life, and your pastoral visiting should suggest many subjects for sermons and help to fill your notebook. When you have visited, for weeks and weeks, some poor lad slowly dying of consumption, or some tired mother of a family ending her hard life in the agony of cancer, you will indeed have misused your time and opportunities if you are not in a position to preach with greater power than before on the uses of suffering and the truth of the psalmist's words: 'It is good for me that I have been in trouble.' The place of pain and sorrow in God's dealings with us, the blessedness of repentance and amendment, the certainty with which, in the long run, God 'gives you back your own,' so that no son who has been good to his mother ever regrets it, no undutiful child but lives to know the bitterness of being a neglected parent—all these are things which should be learned from our daily visiting. And sermons based on experience always go home to the hearts of those who hear them.

If your reading, your recent experiences in visiting, your study of the special needs of the parish or congregation, and the Church's season all fail to suggest an answer to the question, 'What shall I preach about next Sunday?' you can turn to the collect, epistle, and gospel for the week, or to the lessons and psalms. Some people will say that it is to these that you should turn first, since they are the Church's chosen portion for the day. I am not sure of this myself. I suspect that the hardened sermon hearer is often a little put off, at the very outset, when he hears a text selected from the epistle, gospel, or lessons, with the idea that he is going to have a sermon of a more or less formal or conventional type. Whether that is so or not, it is more likely that you will get some valuable suggestion from the appointed portions for the day if you come to them well primed with reading and thought, than if you depend wholly upon them. Indeed, when I have had some subject on which I really wished to preach I have often found, in the epistle or gospel, what seemed just the right text. And it is certainly better to seek a text for something you feel you want to say, than to seek something to say about a text you have selected for no particular reason except that it occurs in the offices for the day.

Some Practical Suggestions

(i) When you have decided on your subject, the next thing is the actual production of the sermon itself. In this connection I would say what a good thing it is to select a subject a good while before the sermon is preached. It is not merely that by so doing you will have longer to think over it and pray over it. It is not merely that during the period of preparation many things in your reading and parochial visiting will probably suggest points and illustrations for the sermon. There is another reason which I am daily more impressed with. Modern writers on psychology are coming to recognise more and more the activity and importance of the subconscious mind, and of what is called unconscious cerebration. Most people have recognised some examples of this unconscious, or semi-conscious, working of the mind. You read a piece of poetry just before going to sleep, and find you know it by heart on waking; the mind has been busy learning it while you slept. You seek in vain for the solution of some difficulty, till at last you put it resolutely away and turn to some other work; when you take up the question again the whole thing seems thought out, clear, and decided by a process of thinking of which you were unconscious. Now all this is obviously a great saving of time and effort. For a specially important sermon, or course of sermons, I often select my topic five or six weeks or more ahead. Then I keep on adding possible points for treatment, or suitable subjects for illustrations, or likely passages of prose or poetry for quotation, without making any effort at selection or arrangement All the matter boils and simmers, so to speak, in my mind for weeks. And then suddenly it sets, so that often, without any conscious effort, I see the whole sermon, or course of sermons, clearly before me, with titles, divisions, sub-divisions, and illustrations as clearly defined as if drawn out on paper. And I have often noticed that the longer a sermon 'simmers' in the mind, and the more suddenly it 'sets,' the better it is. I cannot, of course, be certain that everyone would find this method helpful or indeed possible. But I am sure that the longer we allow a subject to occupy our minds the better, and the more we give the unconscious mind a chance the better.

When you have thought and prayed over your subject either draw up a scheme and then write, or write out the sermon and then analyse. I have given my reasons already for thinking the first the better plan. Then put it away and read it over the next day, or, better still, several days or a week after it was written. You will be in a better position to criticise it then than just after it is finished. When you have preached it, make a note on the back leaf of the date, occasion, and place of preaching. A sermon which is worth preaching once is worth preaching again, and even preaching many times, and often, like good wine, improves with age. But it is an awful thing, when preaching out for a friend or neighbour, to be suddenly smitten with the thought, 'Surely I preached this very sermon here two years ago!'

(ii) To everyone who desires to become a really helpful preacher I would say, 'Preach as often as possible.' It is commonly said that no deacon should be allowed to preach more than once a month during his diaconate. I do not myself agree with this rule. It may be all right for the congregation, who may (though, of course, on the other hand, may not) prefer to hear the vicar. But it is certainly hard on the man keen on learning his job. What is wrong in most parishes is not that young deacons are given too many sermons to prepare, but that they are given too much other work as well, and too little time for study and preparation. If a deacon is allowed, and will loyally use, time for study and preparation, the more he preaches the better. Only by frequent practice will he acquire full control over his powers of expression and delivery, and over his stores of matter.

But it is not enough to preach and speak often. You should aim at doing so to as many different types of people, and under as many different circumstances as possible. Preaching in the open air is splendid practice. If your matter is not interesting, or if it is interesting in itself but not suited to your audience, your congregation will show it in the best and most practical way by walking off and leaving you, a course not open to a congregation in church. So open-air preaching teaches the art of selecting interesting subject-matter, and the yet rarer and more difficult art of suiting your matter to your hearers' conditions and capacities. But open-air preaching, good as its discipline is in respect of matter, is even better in respect of manner. A long, rambling, involved handling of your subject is absolutely fatal. If you are to succeed at all (and, as I have said, you'll soon know, by the behaviour of the listeners, whether you are succeeding or not), you simply must be terse, striking, and easy to follow, as well as audible and simple in language As a foreman in a Yorkshire mill once said to me: 'If you depend on the few who will come on purpose to hear the address, you might as well have stopped in church. That sort would have come to church to hear you. The man you want is the one who is passing by with no thought of stopping to listen. Maybe he's three-quarters of a minute within sound of your voice. If you can't say something that hits him in that time he's gone, not to return. So throw a stone quick and straight and hard, and you'll bag your bird every time.'

Next to open-air preaching I would commend speaking to children, whether in church or in the day and Sunday schools. The same qualities of clearness, vividness in presenting a subject, power in selecting the right topic, and ability to make it interesting, are called for. Of course many people seem to think that a childish manner and infantile matter are what are required with children. That is not so. I never knew a really good preacher to children who was not a first-rate speaker to adults. One of the most helpful teachers and preachers of my time at Cambridge could hold a churchful of poor East London children spellbound. It was only when I heard him do it that I realised where his power with adults lay. So make the most of your opportunities of teaching children, or of preaching to them.

Personally, I am very thankful for the abundant opportunities I had at Leeds of preaching in hospital wards. Such work has many of the advantages of open air and children's work, without the tendency which the latter types of preaching undoubtedly have of betraying us into slangy, free-and-easy, or childish mannerisms. When you stand up in a large ward of sick people you are bound to aim at being simple, interesting, and audible. But surely every man will also feel what a chance it is for a truly evangelical address, and what an opportunity sickness offers for touching the conscience, moving the affections and the will, and 'saying a good word for the Lord Jesus.'

I need not point out how addresses at Band of Hope meetings, short speeches in the middle of a temperance concert, devotional addresses, or instructions and lectures at C.E.M.S. gatherings, all afford opportunities for cultivating a variety of style and manner. Obviously, an address in the middle of a temperance concert wants to be very different to a sermon in church, and it is excellent practice to try and adapt one's address to its time and occasion. But without dwelling in detail on these various kinds of addresses, there is one point I might make. Seize every opportunity of speaking where there is friendly discussion and an opportunity for questions at the close of your speech. It will be a depressing but wholesome discipline to learn how often you have failed utterly to convey your meaning. Often when some thoroughly good fellow, not deficient in general intelligence, has been, in the most friendly and cordial way, expressing his agreement with what he supposes me to have said, I feel inclined to say, 'Is it possible that I can so utterly have failed to convey any idea of what I really meant.'

L

One caution is necessary. When I speak of meetings where questions and discussion are invited, I do not mean public discussions, whether in London or other parks, or in your or your opponents' halls, with secularists or atheists. Whether such discussions ever do any good or not is a debatable point, which we need not try to settle here. But one thing is quite certain, namely, that no young man should engage in such work unless, firstly, he has had ample experience in debating (not, mark you, merely in speaking, but in real debating), and, secondly, unless he has a really strong and capable chairman, otherwise he will be courting failure. The difficulty lies generally, not in the strength of your opponents' arguments, but in their complete inanity. As a very intelligent working man said to me only a few days before this paragraph was written, 'If there was any sense in what those fellows say one could answer them. But who's to answer such stuff as they talk?' But this caution, though a necessary one, has led us far from the subject of preaching.

Alternatives to Sermons

(i) I cannot leave the subject of preaching without saying something of possible alternatives to the usual sermon. And foremost among these comes the simple exposition of Holy Scripture. Sometimes you may really be too busy to prepare a sermon for a weekday service. In that case, instead of giving an unprepared or imperfectly prepared sermon, select a passage of Scripture, say the epistle or gospel for the week or one of the lessons for the day, run through it with a good commentary, and then simply expound it to your people verse by verse. I have never done this without having some expressions of pleasure and gratitude from the congregation afterwards. Our people value their Bibles, but they often fail grievously to understand them, and the continuous exposition of a considerable passage is often more helpful to them than many sermons on detached texts. And if the exposition is simply and suggestively done, it should set the congregation reading their Bibles with renewed zeal. And at the same time, the preparation of such an exposition takes very much less time and trouble and thought than the preparation of an ordinary sermon. It should not take the place of a sermon too often. But from time to time such expositions of a whole chapter, or portion of a chapter, will be valued.

(ii) My last suggestion was meant to help when you are pressed for time. My next certainly has not that advantage. Why do we not more often give our devout weekday congregations a lecture in place of the usual sermon? A really well-prepared lecture may well take much more time in preparation and entail far more reading than many sermons. But for that very reason lectures may be most helpful for our more thoughtful people. What do the books of the prophets Nahum and Habakkuk stand for to most regular church-goers? Or Canticles or the books of Ezra or Nehemiah? It is an excellent thing now and then to substitute for the sermon, on a week-day, or even on a Sunday evening, a lecture on a particular book of Scripture in which you tell what is known or conjectured of the author, sketch the circumstances under which it was written, point out the chief divisions into which it falls, note any passages where the seeming roughness or irrelevance of the text is due to the fact that, though printed in our Bibles as continuous narrative, it is really a dialogue between two characters, and generally make the crooked straight and the rough smooth. Specially valuable are any directions you can give your people as to what they are to look for in their reading. Thus if you tell them to note, in reading Ezekiel, as many examples as possible of his way of illustrating his teaching by dramatic action, or in reading Amos to note the prophet's vivid illustrations drawn from the scenes and incidents of country life, you will set them reading their Bibles keenly and intelligently for themselves. But it must not be supposed that the Old Testament alone offers opportunities for, and requires, such helps to study and appreciation. Lectures on the Gospels, showing the chief characteristics of each, and the circumstances of the writer and those he wrote for, or dealing with the probable history of each Gospel—as in Canon J. J. Scott's admirable little book 'The Making of the Gospels'—are sure to be appreciated. A course of lectures on St. Paul's Epistles is sure to be useful to earnest Bible students. What person who reads these epistles in the order in which they occur in our Bible, and supposes that that is the order in which they were written, can ever hope to understand them or the development of St. Paul's mind? No great wealth of detail is necessary or desirable. It is enough to point out the true chronological order of the epistles, and to show how they fall into four great groups. First, St. Paul is the eager missionary, thinking of little but the conversion of individuals, and their spiritual safety till the dawning of 'that day,' which may be looked for at any moment. But the wholesale fallings away and corruptions of life and faith with which he is confronted, together with a growing experience of what is involved in the evangelisation of a world, make him realise that much of his work needs to be done over again, and better done. So in the second group of epistles (Romans, 1 and 2 Corinthians and Galatians) he lays deep the foundations of the faith, and in that very task is brought face to face with wider and more difficult problems than those of the individual—the problems, that is to say, of society, divine and human, of Church and State. Then he goes to Rome, and the sight of the Imperial City, and the new realisation that it brings of the greatness and majesty of the Roman Empire, bring new conceptions of the nature and work of the Church of Christ. There is a class of continental critic which decries the Pauline authorship of the Epistles to the Ephesians, Philippians, and Colossians, on the ground that they contain ideas foreign to the earlier group. But what sort of a man would it be who could pass from small provincial cities, or even from Antioch and Ephesus, Corinth and Athens, to Rome, and gain no new ideas? If there could be a man so dull and so unimaginative, we can be sure of one thing, St. Paul was not of that type. Finally we see, in the last group, the Pastoral Epistles, the great Apostle as 'Paul the aged,' busied with a thousand practical details of the management of the churches, the reins of government of which he must so soon commit to other hands.

There are many other courses of lectures on books of the New Testament, the Acts, or possibly both Lucan books together, the Johannine books, the Apocalypse by itself, and so on, which will be helpful.

Nor should lectures on doctrine be neglected. A course of the Apostles' Creed might tend to decrease the number of devout Christians who believe that 'descended into hell' means that our Blessed Lord went to the place of the eternally lost. Simple courses on the doctrine of Holy Baptism, the Atonement, the work of the Holy Spirit, the nature of the ministry, and the nature of the Church are obviously called for in these days of universal education and widespread ignorance, when everyone is talking, many are reading, and perhaps not many thinking; or if many are thinking, at any rate many lack the knowledge to make that thinking valuable and fruitful.

Much more difficult, as it seems to me, and certainly less necessary, but not therefore to be despised, are courses of lectures on periods of Church history. Courses on the Oxford Movement, the Evangelical Revival, the Reformation in England or in Europe, the Church of Alexandria, the beginnings of monasticism, the Franciscans and Dominicans, the English mystics, the history of mysticism, the sources of our hymn-book, and a thousand other subjects may be made really interesting and helpful. But there are certain cautions I must offer. It is extremely difficult to strike the happy mean between assuming a background of knowledge in our people which they don't possess, and so making the course both unintelligible and valueless, and, on the other hand, trying to explain everything, and so becoming long, wandering, and tedious, till it is impossible to 'see the wood for trees.' The cure for these evils is to know the subject thoroughly yourself. If, for the purpose of lecturing, you have to cram the subject up in a little handbook, you had far better leave it alone altogether. But if you have really studied your subject, and are then prepared to take some trouble in preparing, digesting, selecting, arranging, and clarifying your matter, you can hardly fail to succeed. For this reason I should not advise a man to try lectures of this type, at any rate in church and to mixed congregations, till he has been five or six years in Holy Orders. And another caution may be added. Do not overdo lectures. Your first duty is to preach the Gospel, and your people's chief need is to be drawn to Christ. A Nonconformist friend told me an apposite story. A minister, earnest, cultured, and scholarly, gave his people plenty of valuable information. One day, going into the pulpit, he found on the pulpit-desk a slip of paper bearing the words, 'Sir, we would see Jesus.' The people felt that their minds were fed and their souls starved. The minister took the hint, and his gospel and evangelical preaching was all the more powerful for being reinforced, but not smothered, with wide reading.

(iii) I cannot close this section without saying a word about the value of practical demonstrations in teaching. For many people teaching, unsupported by practical illustrations, is of little avail. If you want your people to pray, you must not only preach to them about prayer, you must show them how to do it. Sunday evening, when you have a big mixed congregation, is not a suitable time, but on a weekday evening, or at a 'Teaching Mission' in Lent or Advent, it is an excellent thing to preach on prayer, and then to go down and kneel in the centre of the middle aisle (not too far forward, since it is easier for people to hear you when they have their backs to you than when you have your back to them), and pray with a running commentary of reasons and explanations thus:

Let us begin with the Invocation, so as to put ourselves into the presence of God. Say with me, *In the Name of the Father, and of the Son, and of the Holy Ghost.* Let us give the place of honour to Our Lord's own prayer. Say with me the Lord's Prayer. Our best preparation for prayer is confession of sin, general in the morning, detailed in the evening. (Say, as a model, some simple form of confession.) We must never omit thanksgiving for God's undeserved mercies and goodness. (Say, as a model, some simple form of thanksgiving, bringing in as many subjects as possible which will appeal to the people, and suggest topics for private thanksgiving on their part.) We should include 'Acts of Faith,' 'Acts of Love,' and 'Acts of Contrition' in our prayers. (Make such 'Acts' in the simplest language at your control.) We must pray for safety of body and soul, for forgiveness for the past and strength for the future, for wisdom in difficulties, for growth in holiness. (Pray simply, shortly, and so as to bring out the aim of each petition, avoiding vague and conventional phrases.) Let us look ahead and make good resolutions against temptation. (Give examples of such simple practical resolutions as may help your people.)

Another night may be devoted to a demonstration in the art of intercessions. Here you should strive to show how the prayer circle widens from 'my father and mother and brothers and sisters,' or 'my wife and children,' through relations, friends; those I work with—benefactors, enemies, my clergy; those I worship with—the whole parish, the diocese, the mission field, the world. And each head will lend itself to infinite sub-divisions, till your people realise what a great, interesting, and inexhaustible matter intercession is.

And many sermons on meditation may well be less helpful and valuable than one specimen of meditation which you make aloud for your people, showing them how to do it. After such a demonstration of how to pray, how to intercede, how to meditate, I have often had quite well-instructed church people say, 'I really never knew how to set about it before. Books don't seem to help me. Hearing you actually do it was more use than fifty sermons. I hope you'll do something of the kind again. Those who have heard it before won't be sorry to hear it again, and those who have never heard it will be thankful not to miss it. It's just what we want, being shown how to do it.'

A Few General Considerations

(i) This chapter on preaching is already too long, but there are one or two things which I have yet to say. The first is a plea for the dignity of the pulpit. I would most earnestly beg my brethren to avoid common, slovenly, and unworthy language in their sermons. Not every man, of course, has it in his power to become the master of a beautiful and striking style. But there is surely no excuse for men, whose daily duty it is to make use of those twin glories of the English language, the Authorised Version of the Bible and the Collects of our Prayer Book, if they allow their own style to be slipshod, careless, and undistinguished. I do not want 'fine writing' or ornate and florid language, but neither do I care to hear the most sacred subjects discussed in language as common and undistinguished as that of a penny novelette. I may be hypercritical, but I confess that recently a really able sermon was spoilt for me because the preacher ended a carefully worked-out argument with the words : 'Would Jesus have acted so ? No fear. Not a bit of it.' And to speak of our Lord as 'getting right down under the crust' of a subject, or as 'always playing the game,' is to give needless pain to every member of your congregation who has any rudiments of good taste. I am sure I do not exaggerate the prevalence of this evil. I wrote on the topic, some time ago, in a big daily paper, and was overwhelmed with letters. One lady said a clergyman had recently spoken of our Lord as having been 'done in' by the Pharisees, and of Judas and the Pharisees as the men who 'did Him in.' Another told me of the disgust of her son, a young officer in the army, at what the lad, quite truly, called 'the stupid and tactless vulgarity' of the chaplain in calling the centurion's servant the centurion's batman all through his sermon. I think I know what is the cause, or at any rate one of the causes, of the present tendency to slangy and vulgar language in the pulpit. We hear so much nowadays about the clergy being stilted in their manner, and out of touch with the thought of ordinary men, and unable to conform to the ways of men of the world, and so on, and so on, that many good men think to rid themselves of these clerical blemishes by talking as they suppose, quite wrongly, men want them to talk. But if you can't commend the Gospel by plain, straightforward, manly English, you certainly won't by flippant vulgarity and slipshod want of grammar.

And apart from the fallacy of supposing that common language will commend your message, there is another thing to be noted. When a man says startling things, or ordinary things in violent and extravagant language, I always suspect him of being unprepared. I know one man who is a true prophet. But like many prophets his inspiration is intermittent. When 'the Spirit of the Lord is upon him' his language is always simple and dignified, and to listen to him is a privilege and a refreshment. But when he is uninspired he seeks (or seems to me to seek) to gain his accustomed effects by startling sayings. And then his sermons are much talked about but, I suspect, little valued. So, too, I once heard a clergyman tell a mixed congregation that many people thought it a more serious sin to eat peas with a knife than to break the seventh commandment. Half his hearers could not see why they should not eat peas with a knife, or how indeed they could eat them in any other way. The rest were deeply, and I think rightly, pained by a flippant reference to adultery. As you get more and more control over your stores of matter and your method of delivery, you will be able to take greater and greater liberties. And as you get such increased control, your desire to take such liberties will decrease.

Along with vulgarisms and vulgarity in the pulpit, I would venture to protest against cheap vulgarity in advertised titles for courses and sermons. Recently the *Manchester Guardian* contained a noble protest, by their Free Church correspondent, against a man who had advertised a sermon on Jonah under the title 'Three Nights in a Submarine.' And a real leader of thought in our own communion recently preached two sermons in Manchester under the titles 'It Touches the Spot' and 'Insist on seeing the Label,' while even as I write one of the best-known churches in London advertises a course of Lent sermons under the title 'Podsnappery.' Good men, anxious to deliver their message, and full of zeal for their Master, make these mistakes at times. That they are mistakes I am sure.

(ii) Finally, while you will often have to preach to special classes and types of people, avoid preaching to them as classes. Nurses, prisoners, soldiers, sailors, royalty, and all and every other class of people, are just men and women with souls to be saved. If you are preaching a special sermon on the occasion, let us say, of the visit to the parish church of the Butchers' Federation, or the United Fire Brigades of the district, or the Friendly Societies, you will naturally choose your topic accordingly. But nurses in a hospital chapel don't want to hear of nothing but the difficulties and opportunities of a nurse's life, and soldiers and sailors, and kings and criminals, like to be spoken to as men and women only. When it was first my duty to preach in my turn as one of the king's chaplains, one of our spiritual leaders wrote to me, with a kindness I cannot value too highly, and said, 'As for your sermon, try and forget that you are in the chapel at Windsor Castle. Preach a simple sermon about the plain duties of Christian people. Remember the Royal Family are just men and women with souls to be saved.' The advice is good, but good not only for royalty, but for all classes.

CHAPTER V

WORK WITH SPECIAL CLASSES

Children: (i) Manners and methods; (ii) The day schools; (iii) The Sunday school; (iv) Children's services; (v) Ragged Schools; (vi) The Children's Guild; (vii) The Children's Lent Mission.

The Elder Lads: (i) Nature and aims of our work; (ii) Club, Brigade, and Scout Troop; (iii) The holiday camp; (iv) The class in preparation of Communion; (v) Altar-servers.

Girls and Young Women: (i) Need of a strong personal religion; (ii) Character of the work and the worker.

Mothers: (i) The weekday Eucharist; (ii) The women's afternoon service; (iii) The Mothers' Union; (iv) The service for the Feast of the Purification; (v) The Holiday Home.

Men: Need for definite religion.

I WANT in this chapter to deal with the subject of the provision which should be made for different classes of our people, such as children, boys and girls of working age, men and women. Clearly I can only treat these questions in the barest outline. Any one of them might, and probably already has, been made the topic of a whole book. And, again, I have already written of work with boys and with men,[1] and I am unwilling to repeat myself. But some general considerations may, I think, be usefully brought together in this chapter.

[1] 'How to Deal with Lads' (Arnold, *2s. 6d.* net); 'How to Deal with Men' (Arnold, *2s. 6d.* net).

The Children

(i) The importance of gaining and holding our children is admitted by all. Their minds are then indeed 'wax to receive and marble to retain' all impressions. But for that very reason the responsibility of work with children is a serious one, and it is a work where mistakes may do great and lasting harm. The view that 'the vilest abortionist is he who attempts to mould a child's character,' which is apparently growing in popularity, and which counts Mr. George Bernard Shaw among its supporters, appears to me an absurd exaggeration. But there is a measure of truth underlying it. Our duty is to help the character of the child to develop naturally, not to force it into an iron mould which shall turn out child after child of exactly the same pattern, like bricks in a brickfield. I would therefore venture to say, to all workers with children, watch yourselves and see whether you are inclined to favour the quiet docile boy or girl who does everything that you want, and to neglect, or even try to get rid of, the child who won't 'toe the line.' If it is true on the one hand, as I believe it is, that nothing can be effected among children without discipline, and that a rowdy and turbulent Sunday school does more harm than good, it is equally true that, since the only discipline of any moral value is self-discipline, a Sunday school should aim at employing as little repression as possible. What I mean is, that the discipline of the Sunday school should be a thing in which the children gladly and willingly co-operate. Indeed among happy and interested children, who know and are fond of their teachers, the question of discipline should never arise. A Sunday school or other Church organisation from which boys and girls are constantly being expelled, or in which they are constantly being reproved, complained of to parents, or punished, is one the discipline of which needs careful overhauling. Personally, the longer I live the more completely I come to disbelieve in the value of force, or the advantage of making children do what they don't want to do. When I say this in public it never fails to make many of my friends angry. But clearly our duty is to get children to love their religion, and to follow its dictates gladly, not to force them to do what in their hearts they rebel at and dislike. There are requisites for successful work among children, and they are—(*a*) deep respect for the individuality of each child, (*b*) intimate knowledge of each boy and girl, and (*c*) inward quiet of mind on the teacher's own part. The first is the outcome of a prayerful realisation of the infinite variety of human character and the value of a human soul. The second is the necessary prerequisite of all work with human beings, since you can't adapt means to ends unless you know the individuals you are dealing with, and unless they know and trust you. The third requisite is perhaps little understood even nowadays. But anyone may prove its value by experience. I can keep order and gain attention, in any club or class, no matter how big and ill-disciplined, while I maintain inward calm. If I lose control of *myself*, I lose control of my audience. Directly I begin shouting, and saying, 'Sit down, Willie'; 'Tom, be quiet'; 'Albert, if I speak to you again you'll go out,' the case is hopeless. I will quote here a description I have written in another place of the man from whom I first learned this lesson, a lame working man who helped me in quite the roughest and most turbulent Lads' Club I ever knew.

'I think I first learned from him the value, in maintaining discipline over others, of having a tranquil and undisturbed mind oneself. Surely he was the gentlest man that ever lived. In the midst of the racket of the noisiest club he sat quiet and smiling, gentle, genial, and undisturbed. His most severe word of blame for any boy was, "Come, my lad, you don't want to do that, you know." And he never spoke in vain. He once said to me, "They're not bad lads. They mean no harm. I think they're quiet with me along of my lame leg." But it was not his lame leg. It was his gentle mind they recognised.' In dealing with children, then, a man should try to make the free and natural development of the individuality of each boy and girl his chief object. To this end he should seek every opportunity of getting into close intimate touch with his children. And he should strive by all possible means, and especially by prayer, to get a quiet and peaceable mind, so as to avoid a noisy, bullying, dictatorial manner.

(ii) When we consider the various opportunities for work among children, and the best ways of attracting them to church, one thinks naturally of the day schools first. In Lancashire and Yorkshire generally and in the country districts in other parts of England, where Church day schools are still strong, it cannot be denied that they offer the parochial clergy a great opportunity. I use the word 'opportunity' advisedly, for what is offered to the clergy by a good day school is only an opportunity, nothing more, and it is one which can be either used or neglected. If any clergyman supposes that the mere fact that a day school is nominally attached to the parish church, and that the Church Catechism is included in the syllabus of teaching, will draw the scholars in that school into the Sunday school and church, without any efforts of his, he will be grievously mistaken. I have known day schools which were supposed to be models to the whole neighbourhood, the bulk of the children from which attended other Sunday schools, church or chapel. And I have known clergy who were supposed to be leading educationalists who never taught in their own day schools, and scarcely ever visited them except for a managers' meeting or other business occasion. And the two facts are not unconnected.

How, then, may the most be made of the day schools? First and foremost, we must seek a right relation to the teachers. I have heard clergy complain that teachers, especially head teachers, are often touchy and difficult to work with, and not infrequently disloyal. That is certainly not my experience; but if it were so, I really could not wonder. Teachers are educated men and women, very highly trained for a very technical and specialised work, and if they are sometimes suspicious and impatient of the amateur, it cannot be wondered at. And further, the day-school teacher of to-day, working in a Church school, is under the Local Education Authority, and also under the school managers. Now, it is never easy to serve two masters. There is therefore all the greater need that they should not seem to be made subject to a third master, namely, the rector or vicar. I would venture, therefore, to remind my brethren that the parish clergy, simply *qua* clergy, have no authority in the schools whatever. If the teachers need correction or control, it should come from the whole Board of Managers (of which the rector or vicar, though not probably the curate, is likely to be a member) and not from the clergyman. When the parson, vicar, or curate goes in to teach, he goes in primarily as the parson of the parish, not as a manager, and he should do everything possible to show that he feels himself a visitor, welcome doubtless, but still a visitor, on the teachers' ground. The dignity and authority of every teacher, and especially of the head teacher, is a precious asset in a school, and every effort should be made to magnify it in the eyes of the scholars. When the teachers see that the clergy are anxious to consult their wishes, to respect their dignity, and generally to 'magnify their office,' they in turn will be anxious loyally to support their clergy. If I add that new teachers, coming to a district they are unfamiliar with, are often lonely and would welcome friendly relations with the clergy, and that young teachers often have intellectual and spiritual difficulties and would welcome sympathetic help and interest, I clearly suggest something more than merely courteous and correct treatment of our school staffs.

To come to practical details as to the curate's use of the schools. He should, I am sure, teach in the schools one or two mornings a week. Personally, I have never taught any standard below the fifth. It is a curious but undoubted truth, that the younger the children are the harder it is to teach them. The parson therefore, as an untrained amateur, may wisely confine himself to the easiest part of the work. As, too, he cannot teach all classes, he had better take the senior classes, where the scholars will soon be leaving and where they are at, or are approaching, the age for Confirmation. Let him settle with the head teacher what he will teach—Catechism, New Testament, Old Testament, or other subject—and then teach one day a week in the boys' department, and one a week in the girls' department. A third morning may well be devoted to opening the infants' department, hearing the children sing their hymns, or listening while the teacher takes a lesson. Such visits to the infants' department prevent the teachers from feeling neglected. I hope my brethren will not think I harp needlessly on one string if I say that if a clergyman promises to teach, he should be as regular and punctual as one of the regular staff. A curate who is supposed to teach each Tuesday from 9 to 9.45 A.M., and fails to turn up more often than he is present, is simply a nuisance. If illness or unavoidable engagements prevent your teaching, give notice as long before as possible, and let the head teacher decide whether the lesson shall be missed or whether you shall simply change the day that week, giving your lesson on Wednesday or Thursday instead. And if a sudden emergency makes it impossible for you either to attend or give notice of absence, then call at the earliest opportunity and apologise, both to the head teacher and, especially, to the teacher who had to take your place. It is a real hardship on a teacher, who has perhaps counted on a quiet half-hour at the opening of school, to be called on suddenly to take a lesson unprepared.

In one's own teaching it is a mistake to model one's lesson, either in substance or method, too closely on the example of the trained teacher. Your subject is not a secular one; the diocesan examination in religious knowledge is not, or at any rate should not be, like an ordinary examination; finally, your object should be rather to teach religion, as far as that can be taught, than to teach Scripture facts or the text of the catechism. Try to make your lessons stimulating and interesting, so that the children may look forward to them while they are at school, and back to them with pleasure after they have left. If you want to maintain order and discipline, and not merely to rely on the discipline of the school, you must know your scholars individually. Visit the parents of your day school class as regularly as those of your Sunday school children, whether they attend church or not. It is also an excellent thing to interest yourself in the school games, going with the senior boys when they are taken, in school hours, to the public swimming-baths, or watching the school cricket or football team after school hours.

It is certainly desirable that the school as a whole should be brought into church from time to time, say on saints' days or one day a week in Lent. This, by arrangement with the Local Education Authority, can be done during the time set apart for religious instruction, which may be either at the beginning or the end of the session. I cannot help thinking that a school which never goes, as a corporate body, to church misses a great opportunity. As a visit to the local museum, or cathedral, or other object of interest does more, by its appeal to the eye and by the awakening of interest, than any number of lessons in school to stimulate interest in history or any kindred topic, so a service in church has more effect on the children than any amount of talking about religion to them.

Where the teachers live near the school and church they are often willing to bring the children to church, out of school hours, in Lent or at the time of a mission. Then the question arises whether to have them come to church straight from school, in which case you will get the bulk of them, but they will be tired and bored, or to let them go home to tea and return at a later hour, when you will get fewer, but they will be fresher and keener. Whichever you elect for, it is quite clear that it is no part of the teachers' duties to bring the children, and any who don't feel inclined to do so should not be made to feel uncomfortable by their refusal.

The annual sermons in aid of the day schools—what in the North we call the Day School Anniversary—the Christmas parties, the annual school concert, or prize giving, when the children perform, and similar functions, may all be made valuable opportunities of interesting the parents, not only in the education of their children, but in the Church. There is no point of attack for working-class people better than the children. The curate who is good with the children will find his difficulties few and easily overcome.

(iii) While the day schools, where there are any, must necessarily be the best recruiting ground for the Church, it is the Sunday school in which the really important training must be given. Now I do not hesitate to say that there is no department of Church work in which a newly arrived curate can do as much and as lasting harm as in the Sunday school if he is hasty, arbitrary, tactless, and inconsiderate. If, that is to say, he fails in the spirit of Christ. A keen man comes, let us suppose, to a parish and wants to take the class for senior lads. He is sure he could get better results of church attendance, Confirmation, and Communion than are being got. But he finds some uncompromising old gentleman, with grey whiskers and an unpleasant manner, who has taken the class for five-and-forty years. Or he finds a large but ill-arranged and disorderly Sunday school, and is certain that if he started the service of the Catechism in church every Sunday it would yield better results, but he finds the bulk of the teachers steadily set against any change. Or, again, he finds a Sunday school from which few scholars come forward for Confirmation, and where there is at best an annual service in church, and he proposes a monthly service in church, which the teachers all protest against. If in such a case the vicar is one who, either through slackness or pressure of other work, takes little interest in the Sunday schools and believes in 'giving his colleague a free hand,' a curate is much tempted to force his plans on the school. What happens? The old Bible Class teacher, after years of faithful if not always highly efficient service, leaves, and the young men who were the first to make fun of his peculiarities resent the way he has been treated and themselves stay away. Or the teachers, rebellious at having their work condemned as inefficient, leave in a body or become irregular and lacking in enthusiasm. And the whole Sunday school suffers. Probably at the end of a couple of years the curate himself realises that the work is not prospering, and decides to seek a more congenial sphere. But it is one thing to drive people away and quite another thing to bring them back again, and the reformer's successor, no matter how zealous and tactful, will perhaps never succeed in restoring the harmony and prosperity of the school. One thing every clergyman, and especially every curate, should remember, namely, that he is more or less temporary, while the people are, or should be, as compared with him, permanent. Where changes, reforms, development are to be attempted, it should be done slowly, after due discussion and with the full consent of the teachers. If a man is seen to be keen, a real worker, with the love of Christ, and of Christ's little ones, in his heart, he will soon find the teachers ready to support him and to consent to the changes he wants. And where they won't agree to his changes, it may well be because they are right and he is wrong—because, that is to say, they know and understand local conditions and local prejudices and he does not. No man, for instance, fresh from the South can understand at first North-country feeling about Sunday school, any more than a Yorkshireman or Lancashireman, used to men and women going on at 'school' till past middle age, can understand straight off what is necessary to hold the London boy or girl to church once they have left the day school. The new curate, therefore, should be willing, and should show that he is willing, to be guided by the opinion of his teachers. Not of this or that teacher or clique, but of the whole body of teachers expressed through the teachers' meeting. If there is an active and popular superintendent, let the curate be content to teach the senior boys' class. If the senior boys' class has long been taken by one and the same teacher, let the curate be content to superintend. Often a clergyman can do more good by taking a class a little below the highest, say the boys of fourteen to fifteen years, than by taking the senior lads of seventeen to eighteen years or the Young Men's Bible Class. Let him be ready to go where he is most needed, and do the work which most wants doing. That is how he will secure the most influence in the school.

There is so plentiful a literature on Sunday school work and method, that there is no need for me to go into details. But there are one or two points which, if I may trust my experience, are too little noted. Most books on Sunday school work assume perfect conditions, adequate room, sufficient apparatus, and competent, if not ideally perfect, teachers. But the ordinary parish falls far short of such perfection. Many Sunday schools are fearfully overcrowded, most are too poor to buy anything like all the apparatus of lesson-books, maps, pictures, etc., described in text-books on the reformed Sunday school, and almost all have at least some teachers on the staff who lack all qualifications for their work except self-sacrificing zeal. Well, it seems to me to be our duty to do the best we can with imperfect conditions. I have heard a zealous lecturer on Sunday school reform urge a clergyman to get rid of nine-tenths of the children in the school, so that the rest might be taught under better conditions. 'Far better,' he declared, 'do a small work really well than a big work badly. If you confine yourself to a tenth of your present number you will be training teachers for the next generation.' This sounds very plausible, and I have not room here to discuss the pros and cons of the subject. I will only say that I am whole-heartedly on the opposite side. Never turn a child away if it can be avoided. Never let a child go if it can be retained. Perfect conditions do not always yield perfect results even in secular teaching, and the Sunday school aims at teaching not mere Bible history, but religion. If the right spirit, the spirit of love for God and for the children, is present, splendid work may be done under the worst conditions. I am no opponent, far from it, of Sunday school reform, for improved conditions of teaching and better apparatus are things to be desired. But our duty is to make the best possible use of what we have, and not to be discouraged.

There is, however, one condition necessary for good work, which the curate should work for unceasingly. It is good order and discipline—discipline alike among the scholars and the teachers. Children are always most troublesome when they are bored. Indeed, I might almost say that they are never ill-behaved except when bored. But there can be nothing but boredom where all is noise, confusion, reprimands, complaints, and punishments. The things which make for order are teachers who come filled with, and calmed by, prayer; teachers in their places before the scholars begin to come in, opening prayers taken quietly, reverently, and impressively, lessons well prepared and brightly delivered, and an atmosphere of sympathetic understanding between scholars and teachers. If, on the other hand, a thoroughly disorderly Sunday school is wanted, it is easy to state the receipt for its production. Let the teachers arrive hot and breathless when the scholars have been rushing about the room for some ten minutes. Let an inadequate supply of torn hymn-books be distributed and struggled for. Let the superintendent select a hymn at random, remember that it was sung the week before and possibly the week before that, and select another, only to find that it is torn out of the music copy on the harmonium, or that no one present can play. Let him punctuate his work with shouts of 'Children, be quiet'; 'Mr. Brown, will you please keep your boys quiet'; 'Boys, I will not have this disorder'; 'What are the senior girls doing?' and so on. Finally, let several boys be turned out, or even ejected struggling, and the effect will be complete.

If any boy is reported as incorrigible, the best thing is for the curate to have him in some week night for a friendly talk. Not a solemn lecture, in which the object is to make the boy feel ashamed of himself, but a friendly talk, the object of which is to restore the boy's self-respect if he already feels ashamed of himself, and to remove the feeling of soreness and irritation if he feels—as boys often do in such cases—that he has been hardly treated. Many, indeed most boys, have their foolish fits between the ages of fourteen and sixteen, and can then be extraordinarily provoking and silly. But it is ten thousand pities to lose a boy for good just for lack of a little patience at the critical time. It is strange, but a lady often deals with lads of this age better than a man. At any rate scholars, whether boys or girls, must not be expelled. Often a troublesome boy can be best dealt with by finding him a job of work.

(iv) I am sure that we have not yet solved the problem of Sunday services for children. The children's service in church which has to be got in between half-past nine, which is the earliest possible if the curate is to get any breakfast, and quarter-past ten, which is the latest hour if the general congregation are to get into church by 10.30 A.M., the usual hour in the North, is unsatisfactory, not so much because the time is too short, for I am sure that no service, for children only, should much exceed forty-five minutes in length, but because it is the wrong service at the wrong time. It is the wrong service because it cuts them off from, instead of uniting them to, the general congregation. And it is at the wrong time because it turns them loose at the most inconvenient time for the parents. The parochial sung Eucharist, where that is established, is, I am sure, the right service for children. If the sermon is short, as it should be in the morning, and the music not too elaborate, the service should not last more than an hour and a quarter, or less, and the children will learn to love it. When I am asked why I advocate the presence of young children at a sung Eucharist, I always avoid theological arguments, and rest on one fact of which my own experience has convinced me. When the children attend Mattins and go out before the sermon, or where they go out with the bulk of the congregation at the Prayer for the Church Militant, it is extremely difficult to get boys and girls to offer themselves for Confirmation, and they lapse readily from Communion afterwards. Where the children are accustomed to being present at a sung Eucharist there is no question of getting children to offer for Confirmation, for they come forward quite unasked and sometimes need rather to be checked than urged, and they readily become regular and consistent communicants. The reason is obvious. In the first case, the service is wholly unfamiliar, and partaking of Holy Communion is regarded at best as the privilege of a few exceptional saints, and at worst as the peculiarity of a few stuffy old men and women, who like to stay on in church when the great bulk of the people are glad enough to be released. In the second case, where, that is to say, attendance at the sung Eucharist is the rule, the service is familiar from the child's earliest days, and Communion takes its right place as an integral part of the life of every adult Christian. But the question of an evening service for children is less easy. The sermon at Evensong is one of the great opportunities of teaching the general congregation, and though it should seldom if ever exceed half an hour, it may, and I think should, usually approximate to that length. But Evensong with a half-hour's sermon is no service for young children. Yet what are working people to do if they have young children and can't bring them to church with them? Personally, I am a great believer in a well-organised children's service conducted in a school or mission hall at the time of the parish church Evensong. It should be a liturgical service modelled as closely as possible on the Prayer Book, so as to form a real training in, and introduction to, liturgical worship. Everything should be done to give the room where it is held the appearance of a church, and reverence should be a chief matter aimed at. Finally, the children should take as full a part as possible, not only in the service, but in the management. Let there be a children's choir, let one of the senior scholars read the lessons, let there be church officers elected. I have often longed for a parish where it would be possible to hold, in a district church, a crypt, or other building, a true 'Young People's Church' with its morning and evening service for, and wholly in the hands of, young people under eighteen years old. The priest would be the only adult. But that is a council of perfection. One difficulty of children's services everywhere is the presence of very young children. If you exclude all children under, say, seven years old, many elder children are kept away because they are expected to mind their younger brothers and sisters. And really you can't blame the parents. A working woman who has been hampered, all school time, by a couple of children of five and three, or a mother with a baby in arms who has also a child of three or four able to run about and get into all sorts of mischief and danger, naturally looks to the elder children to take them off her hands out of school hours. Not to recognise the reasonableness of this is to alienate the mother's sympathy and interest at once. How often do we hear a tired mother say, 'If our Emma can't bring the little one to the service, she'll just have to bide at home herself. I can't be moithered with the childer myself after having them all day.' On the other hand, the presence of a large number of what a fellow curate of mine used to call 'crawlers' upsets any service. There is no solution for this problem, unless a special room, in which babies may be left under the charge of helpers, can be provided. Personally, I always admit 'crawlers.' It is an excellent discipline for the preacher, and if he can hold his congregation under such circumstances it is a triumph.

(v) In connection with Sunday schools and children's services, I must say something about what are usually called Ragged Schools. I dislike the title, much preferring the name Sunday Night School, but I am an intense believer in the thing itself. Indeed, there are many parishes in which it is quite impossible for the Church to do her duty without a Sunday Night School. In many, perhaps in most, working-class parishes there are some streets of a distinctly poorer class than the rest. The children from these streets, whether because of class distinctions which escape our notice, or because of their lack of Sunday clothes, or for some other reason, simply will not come to the ordinary afternoon Sunday school. But they will come to an evening Ragged School. I shall perhaps best make my point clear by describing my own experiences with Ragged Schools. There was an excellent one in my first parish, managed by a zealous young layman. But as it met at the time of Evensong, I saw little of it beyond the annual prize giving. In my present parish also I found a flourishing Night School most zealously served by male and female teachers. But as it met from 5.30 to 6.30 P.M., a most inconvenient time for a busy clergyman, I had little actual experience with it. A few months after the declaration of war, however, it was clear that either I must take the senior boys' class or it must be closed down. I therefore took the class, and at the moment of writing I have a class of about seventy-five little boys, of from twelve to fifteen, of the paper-boy type. In the winter months I get an average attendance of sixty; in the summer it drops to perhaps half that number. And few drop off altogether. And, after nearly five years of it, I can say without hesitation that taking the class is the most interesting, the pleasantest, and I believe in many ways the most valuable work I do. It has brought me into pleasant relations not only with a type of boy whom I should never have met in the ordinary Sunday school, but also with their parents and homes. The class has yielded a good proportion of boys who attend church, a fair proportion of Confirmation candidates, and several altar-servers. But best of all, it has solved, or at least opened a way to the solution of, the problem of the poorest streets and homes which the Church seemed powerless to touch. Of course the way in which the class is conducted is different from that of an ordinary Sunday school or Bible Class. My own plan is as follows—hymn, prayers, which always include one or more collects which the boys know by heart and repeat all together, and an extempore prayer, bringing in references to sick members, parents, or relations who have died recently, and similar topics, a second hymn, a short lesson on some Bible or other religious subject, and a story. The story is a great feature. After many experiments I found that what the boys like best is a public school story. Anyone with a little invention can make them up for himself. Any publisher who is prepared to make me a generous offer can have a volume, 'The Best Fag at Stockleigh, and other Public School Tales,' all of which have passed the test of being told to my Ragged School.

The annual prize giving is a great opportunity. The parents come, many of them of the type it is hardest to get to any religious service or meeting.

A good layman to give a short address, a kind lady to give the prizes, a speech from the conductor of the class on its objects, with an appeal for the interest and co-operation of the parents, a couple of sacred songs by a voluntary singer, plenty of hymns by the scholars, and the usual prayers and Bible reading make up the programme. Many people complain that Ragged Schools are purely undenominational, and do nothing to attach children to their church. That is, and will remain, true as long as the clergy take little or no interest in them, and the Church generally leaves them to zealous Nonconformists. I would urge every curate in a poor parish to interest himself in the Sunday Night School if there is one, and to start one if there is none. The work will call out the zeal and enthusiasm of many young men and women who will offer themselves as teachers, and if the curate himself teaches a class, he will find the Ragged School boy, as I have found him, a delightful little fellow.

(vi) The next subject calling for attention in connection with children's work is the Children's Guild. I am sure it is a mistake to have too many organisations for children in a parish. If you have a Band of Hope, a Young People's Missionary Society, a Guild of the Good Shepherd, a Band of Mercy, and perhaps half a dozen other guilds and societies, you get the same children, more or less, at each, and the whole thing is overdone. Much better have one Children's Guild which can devote one night a month to temperance, one to missions, one to kindness to animals, and so on. The activities of a well-managed Band of Hope, the wood-work, basket-work, and other classes in manual work, the organised games, morris dancing, and singing, and the preparation of a missionary pageant, a missionary exhibition, or missionary sale of work, will keep the children happy and interested all the year round, and find congenial work for all sorts of helpers. Here, again, the interest and co-operation of the parents should be sought. It is a good thing that all the happiest and brightest memories of childhood should be connected with church.

If, as is highly probable, the Ragged School children and Sunday school children won't mix in the Guild, a Pleasant Evening should be run on another night if a room and helpers can be found. We have the Children's Guild on Mondays and the Happy Evening on Wednesdays, and there is an automatic classification. Few of the Ragged School attend the former, few of the Sunday school the latter. The Pleasant Evening offers singing, simple needlework, and games to the girls, and games and romping to the boys.

(vii) I cannot leave the subject of the children without saying a word about the Children's Lent Mission. Most well-worked parishes nowadays make some provision for the adult congregation in Lent by means of special services, or special courses of sermons. But often too little is done for the children. Yet a special effort for children in Lent is most valuable, and something striking should be aimed at. One excellent plan I learned from the Rev. C. H. Rolt, now Dean of Capetown, who used it at all children's missions during the Mission of Help to South Africa in 1904. Suppose there is a service for children once a week during the six weeks of Lent. In that case a series of six coloured cards is printed of six different colours, the card being about 3½ inches by 2½ inches. The series that lies before me as I write is printed on pink, mauve, yellow, blue, green, and scarlet cards. I give an exact copy of the first card.

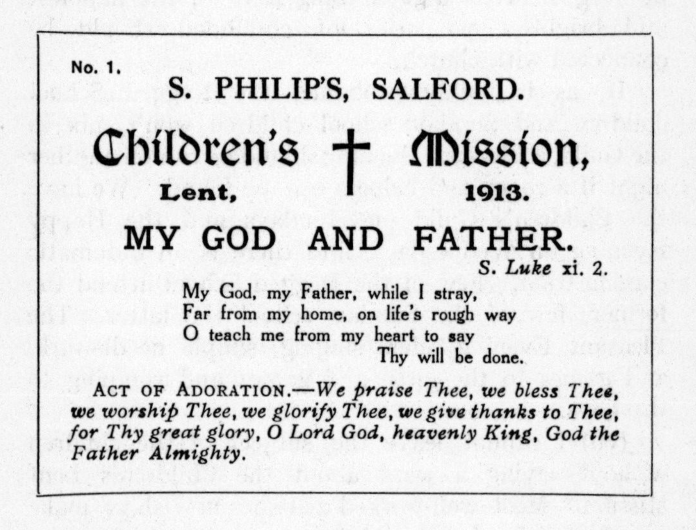

No. 1.

S. PHILIP'S, SALFORD.

Children's † Mission,

Lent, 1913.

MY GOD AND FATHER.

S. Luke xi. 2.

My God, my Father, while I stray,
Far from my home, on life's rough way
O teach me from my heart to say
Thy will be done.

ACT OF ADORATION.—*We praise Thee, we bless Thee, we worship Thee, we glorify Thee, we give thanks to Thee, for Thy great glory, O Lord God, heavenly King, God the Father Almighty.*

The remaining five are as follows:

(2) My Soul; S. Mark viii. 36–37. Verse, 'Awake, my soul, and with the sun.' Act of Faith, 'I believe in God the Father, Who has created my soul. I believe in God the Son, Who has redeemed my soul. I believe in God the Holy Ghost, Who sanctifies my soul.'

(3) My Sins; 1 S. John i. 8–9. Verse, 'All my sins uprising now.' Act of Confession, 'O my Father, I have sinned against Heaven and before Thee, and am no more worthy to be called Thy son.'

(4) My Saviour; S. John iii. 16. Verse, 'Glory be to Jesus.' Act of Contrition, 'O my God, I am truly sorry for all my sins. O make me love Thee more and more.'

(5) My Comforter; S. John xiv. 26. Verse, 'Thou of Comforters the best' (from Hymn 156, A. & M.). Act of Prayer, 'Come, Holy Ghost, and fill the hearts of Thy faithful people, and kindle in them the fire of Thy love.'

(6) My Worship; Ps. xcv. 6. Verse, 'To Thy temple I repair; Lord, I love to worship there; When within the veil I meet Christ before the mercy-seat.' Act of Self-dedication, 'And here we offer and present unto Thee, O Lord, ourselves, our souls and bodies, to be a reasonable, holy, and lively sacrifice unto Thee.'

Each child receives a card, and there is always great keenness not to miss one of the series. This makes it possible to give a consecutive series of instructions, which is just what our children require. And as the various 'acts' of adoration, faith, confession, etc., are learned by heart and repeated all together, there is a real impression made on the children's minds.

As it does not do to repeat such a thing as these cards two years' running, lest the effect should be spoilt, I have tried to vary it as much as possible. In Lent, 1915, I used what was called 'The Soldier's Pocket Book.' A piece of cardboard six inches by five inches was folded to form a booklet. On the outer side, which was khaki coloured, was printed as follows:

S. Philip's, Salford

THE SOLDIER'S
POCKET BOOK

Issued to......................

✠

Lent 1915

Inside it was printed as on opposite page.

Then at each service every child was given a small slip, printed on gummed paper, which bore the special teaching of the day, and could be stuck into the space reserved for it in the pocket-book. The slips were printed as follows:

(1) *The Enlistment.*—'Endure hardness, as a good soldier of Jesus Christ,' 2 Tim. ii. 3. I am a soldier in God's army; I must be loyal to my Captain.

(2) *The Training.*—'Take the helmet of salvation, and the sword of the Spirit,' Eph. vi. 17. I am a soldier in God's army; I must learn to use my weapons.

(3) *On Guard.*—'Watch and pray, that ye enter not into temptation,' St. Matt. xxvi. 41. I am a soldier in God's army; I must stand my guard.

(4) *In the Battle.*—'Watch ye, stand fast in the faith, quit you like men, be strong,' 1 Cor. xvi. 13. I am a soldier in God's army; I must expect hard fights.

(5) *Wounded.*—'I will heal thee of thy wounds, saith

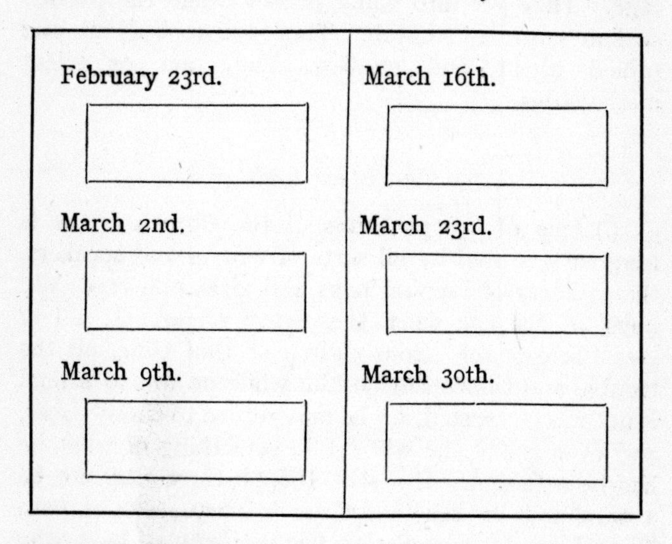

the Lord,' Jer. xxx. 17. I am a soldier in God's army; if I am wounded He will heal me.

(6) *Victory.*—'Be thou faithful unto death, and I will give thee a crown of life.' I am a soldier in God's army; I must not grow weary, but fight bravely to the end.

Other plans were tried in other years, and experience proves that any particular device can be repeated after an interval of five or six years, but not sooner.

The object is at once to attract the children to the service, to give an opportunity for consecutive teaching on such subjects as sin, repentance, prayer, worship, etc., and to fix the teaching given in their minds. But such devices as the coloured cards and the 'Soldier's Pocket Book' have another advantage. They get into many houses where the parents seldom come to church. They are looked at, and talked about, and studied. They act as silent missionaries.

The Elder Lads

(i) One of the problems of the Church is, as is frequently stated by all sorts of writers and speakers, the problem of keeping boys and girls, and especially boys, at the age when they leave school. If a boy gets 'broken off' from church at that time, all the trouble and time spent on him while he was at school is not wholly wasted, for he may return to church later, and even if not, he will retain something of what he has been taught. But still, though there may not be a total loss to religion, there is very grievous loss. Now, I am convinced that the majority of boys who are lost to the Church are lost through failure of patience and sympathetic understanding on the part of those who have to deal with them. Most boys under fourteen are sensible, serious, and manageable. Nearly all boys, some time between fourteen and seventeen, pass through an awkward period (their 'lout' stage, as one old lady of my acquaintance calls it), when they are very difficult to manage.

They are too old to be nice little boys, and too young to be pleasant young men. Also they are impatient of restraint, and touchy on the subject of their dignity. A very little undue harshness and severity on the part of a lad's teacher or clergyman, a very little impatience and lack of understanding, and the boy is lost to the Church. It may be that the choir-master complains that he can do nothing with the lad, or the Sunday school teacher insists that he shall be expelled from Sunday school as not merely disorderly, but the cause of disorder in others, or the wardens complain of him and his companions for getting into back seats of the side aisles or gallery and behaving badly. Now I am not suggesting that the just complaints of these workers should be ignored. But I do say that the one vital thing is that a boy who is silly and not bad, and who in a few years will have grown into a really valuable church worker, should not be lost to the Church for lack of a little patience and common sense. In such cases I personally always adopt one course. To the angry choir-master, teacher, or warden I point out the vital importance of keeping the lads to church, and the need for patience. Sometimes also, since it is young men who are usually the sternest disciplinarians, I remind the complainer that five years ago there was no greater nuisance, nor anyone more often complained of, than himself. To the boy I say, in a friendly talk in my own room, that I am sure he's not bad, but merely silly; that if he must be silly, I wish he would try not to be any sillier than he can help, and that in the meanwhile it is I who suffer, since the church officers say I manage the boys badly. I have written at some length on this subject, because I am sure that every year thousands of lads are lost to the Church for lack of a little patience and common sense. The boys go off feeling sore and resentful, since they are not conscious of any particular wrong-doing. The clergy and church workers are sore and resentful, since they feel that children they have spent time and trouble over have turned out badly and proved ungrateful. The only cure is intimate knowledge of our boys and girls (for what I have written is, I believe, as true of the girls as of the boys), and real sympathy and affection for them.

Before leaving this section I must say one word more. Does the Church recognise adequately the services of her choir boys? What proportion of our choir boys, after giving their services freely for years, either drift out of the choir unnoticed or leave in anger? I am thinking of a lad now who after six years zealous work as a choir boy was seen by the curate laughing during the vestry prayer. As there had been trouble with him before, he was told to take off his surplice and cassock and leave the church. He did so and, as leading boy, felt deeply disgraced. Nothing that the clergy or his parents could do could get him back to church. He was fifteen at the time, and his next appearance in any church was when he came on leave, aged twenty-three, having been confirmed in France. Can anyone blame the lad or deny that his services to the Church were ill-requited? It is an excellent thing to have a rule that every boy who leaves the choir with honour after five years' service should receive a really handsome Bible or other suitable book. Here is a copy of the inscription I last signed:

Presented to A. B., for seven years a zealous and valued member of the choir of St. Philip's, Salford, and for two years senior boy and leading treble soloist.

PETER GREEN, *Rector.*
A BLANK } *Churchwardens.*
J. DASH }

Even if the expense is heavy it is, looked at from the lowest point of view, a sound business investment.

(ii) It has been remarked above that the chief thing needed is a real knowledge of one's boys. I cannot deal with work among lads in detail here. I tried to do so fifteen years ago in my little book 'How to Deal with Lads,' and I feel bound to say that after fifteen years more of work with lads there is nothing I want to alter, and little I want to add to, in that book. But there are one or two things I should like to say. Firstly, I am convinced that the sole end and aim of all organisations—Club, Brigade, Scout troop, or what not—is to give the worker a chance to get to know, and be known by, his boys. 'I know My sheep and am known of Mine' is a full treatise on the essentials of the pastoral office. Secondly, I am convinced that it really matters very little what organisation you select. One man will like, and be able to use to advantage, the comparative liberty of a club. Another will prefer the discipline of the Church Lads' Brigade. But the thing that matters is the man rather than the organisation. I have had certain organisations recommended to me, because they 'don't depend on the character of the man in charge. Anyone can run the work. You don't need a man specially good with boys.' I am deeply convinced that this is a delusion. The Americans have a saying that 'there's no machine that is fool-proof.' Equally there is no organisation for boys that is fool-proof. If a man is fussy, bossy, dictatorial, and lacking in sympathy on the one hand, or if he is weak, slack, and sentimental, keen for a week and careless for a month, on the other hand, he'll wreck the work. Beyond that, I can only say that each man must choose the weapon he prefers. I like a Lads' Club best. Of the rival organisations of Brigade and Scouts, I am inclined to think that the Brigade enables a man to handle the greater number of lads in a given time and at a given cost, while a Scout troop offers the best opportunities for intensive work with a smaller number. With all organisations beware of putting the success of the Club, or Brigade, or Troop above the welfare of the individual. The organisation exists for the lad, not the lad for the organisation. I have given elsewhere my reasons for believing that all organisations connected with the Church should be on a definitely religious basis.

(iii) There is one means of getting to know one's lads which is of unique value. I mean the camp. Many people think this means an expensive and elaborate affair, with tents, feeding marquees, professional arrangements for sanitation, and all the difficulties of finding a suitable camping ground.

That is not so. For the last nine years I have spent Whitsun week in camp with parties of from fifty or eighty lads with none of these difficulties. All that is necessary is an old house, empty school, disused chapel, or suitable parish room which will supply us with a room to sleep in, a room for meals, some sufficient sanitary accommodation, and a kitchen or room where a gas stove can be fixed. Each member receives a palliasse filled with straw, extra straw for the pillow-case he brings himself, and two army blankets. A camp-bed can be hired for a shilling or two extra by any whose bones are too old for the floor. There is no officers' mess, and no officers' dormitory. All take their share in orderly duties, such as sweeping out the dormitory, fetching milk, peeling potatoes, serving meals. The actual cooking is done by two senior members of the Girls' Club, who act as voluntary W.A.A.C.'s and lodge near the camp. Senior members of the congregation, wardens, sidesmen, and other adults, often spend the week, or part of it, in camp, and married couples take lodgings near for the pleasure of having meals at the camp and sharing its life. It is an advantage to have it in or near a town rather than in a too remote village. Thus Southport proved more successful than Hoylake, and Hoylake than Thurstaston. The close association of men and lads of all ages, from the rector and the people's warden at one end to the twelve year old boys from the Ragged School at the other, is of infinite value. This year our organist, who has always been admirable with the choir boys, and who has kept in close touch with the senior lads by means of a minstrel troupe, said to me, 'I feel as if I had never really known or understood the lads till I had this week in camp with them. It's been a revelation.' That is true.

Each member pays his own railway fare, and a sum which varies from 5*s.* 6*d.* for boys under fourteen to 21*s.* for men over twenty-one for food. But many boys cycle to the camp and so save train fares, and others, whose fathers work on the railway, get privilege tickets. Here is the balance-sheet for the 1918 camp at Southport :

Receipts.	£	*s.*	*d.*	*Expenditure.*	£	*s.*	*d.*
By balance from 1917	0	9	7	By railway . .	12	7	0
,, Members' payments	38	15	6	,, Printing and postages . .	0	14	0
,, Proceeds of dance	4	14	3	,, Cooks' lodgings .	0	10	0
,, ,, ,, concert	11	14	5	,, Donation to cooks	2	0	0
,, Collection for helpers . .	0	16	6	,, Straw . .	0	10	0
,, Sale of food .	2	8	11	,, Hall rent . .	4	0	0
,, Subscriptions .	7	17	6	,, Breakages . .	0	13	0
				,, Sundries . .	3	16	9
				,, Tips . . .	0	9	10
				,, Gas . . .	0	15	0
				,, Coal . . .	0	5	0
				,, Hire of beds .	1	2	6
				,, Railway carriage	0	15	1
				,, Groceries . .	37	13	6
				,, Balance in hand	1	5	0
	£66	16	8		£66	16	8

Nothing is put down for meat, as a wholesale butcher in the market presented us with a whole sheep, which two butchers, members of the club, cut up as required. And there were other gifts, such as 40 lb. of Quaker Oats. On the other hand, such things as were paid for were very costly in 1918. It is safe to say that nearly seventy lads and men could not have got a week's holiday in Southport for anything like so cheap a rate in any other way.

(iv) While thinking of camp, club, and brigade, we must never lose sight of the fact that religion is the thing we are out for. The boy or girl whom we do not bring to a knowledge of Christ as Saviour, to a real love of religion for its own sake, and to active membership of the Church, is a boy or girl with whom we have failed. And I am deeply convinced that we clergy often fail through not making this plain. We do really desire to win our young people for Christ, but we think we shall best do so by not obtruding religion. The exact opposite is the truth. Our people often wonder whether we really care about their souls. And though their doubts may be unjustified in reality, they are often not without excuse, owing to our reserve. I would therefore say, to every young curate just beginning work, Don't be always ramming religion down people's throats at inopportune times, but make it clear to all your people, and especially your boys and girls, that you are God's man intent on God's work, and that you are out to make 'faithful soldiers and servants' of Christ. Now the secret of success with young people is regularity and teaching. What we want is for our young people to form habits of prayer, Bible study, church-going, and Communion, and that steady teaching should secure that such habits are intelligent. Therefore the Lads' Bible Class, the Senior Girls' Class, and the monthly class for lads in preparation for Holy Communion, and the similar monthly class for girls, are of absolutely vital importance. Almost anything should be neglected sooner than these. I have known many boys and girls whose excuse for having 'got broken off from church' was that they 'went Sunday after Sunday and there was never anyone to take the class.' And many young people simply will not come to Communion without the help of a class in preparation. Many clergy have spoken to me of the difficulty of getting young people, especially lads and young men, to a preparation class on a week night, and of their discouragement when, month after month, only one boy, or at most three or four, turn up. Now, since truth is naturally one's first object in such a book as this, I shall, I hope, be forgiven if I say plainly that I have never found any difficulty. Hence if you find a difficulty consider the following points:

(*a*) *Is the hour wrong or the night ill-chosen?* Friday is almost impossible for working girls in the North. It is the night when they are expected to do house work. Certain nights in the week are Night School nights for the boys. Personally, I have found Monday the best night for girls and Friday for lads, but the nights vary in different districts. Eight o'clock is about the worst possible hour. If a boy or girl has finished tea by six o'clock or soon after, an eight o'clock engagement, even if it only lasts twenty minutes, cuts up the whole evening. Can a boy be expected to leave the cricket-field while there are two more full hours of playing light—as there are in these days of summer time—or to leave the club in the middle of the evening and so lose his turn on the billiard table? I have found 8.45 or 9 P.M. for girls, and 9.15 P.M. or 9.30 P.M. for boys good times. If the class lasts twenty to twenty-five minutes, they will be out in time to meet unconfirmed friends leaving the Girls' Club at 9.30 P.M. or the Lads' Club at 10 P.M. I have laboured this point, for the success or failure of the class may turn on just such a detail.

(*b*) *Is the class held regularly?* If the right hour has been chosen and the class still is a failure, is it because it is held irregularly and any and every excuse is accepted for dropping it? It cannot be too often repeated that with young people regularity is what tells. Don't say, 'Oh, we had a special service in church on the lads' night this month, so I asked them to attend that instead of a preparation class.' The late hour for the class ought to make it possible to avoid clashing. Personally, the first thing I do when I get my new diary each year is to enter the Lads' Preparation Class on the Friday before each first Sunday in the month, and the Girls' Preparation Class on the Monday before each fourth Sunday in the month. And as the class should be held regularly, so the notices should be sent out regularly. The difference in effectiveness between a notice given out in church or Bible Class and a written notice received by the individual boy or girl is so great as to make the extra trouble well worth while. And I find a cyclostyled letter, which can be varied each month, is more effective than a printed card on which the date alone is left blank and filled in for each month. And if such notices are usually sent by post, or taken out by the Scouts, it will have a very good effect for the clergyman in charge of the class to deliver them personally every three months or so.

(*c*) *Is there an apparent prejudice against the class?* Sometimes there seems to be a prejudice against such a class, so that from the first there is no response to the clergyman's efforts. This may be met as follows. Get ten or a dozen of the best lads or girls together, tell them of the value and importance of the class, and ask them to help you by trying to be at the monthly class every month without missing once till the next year's Confirmation candidates have been confirmed and are ready to join. Such newly confirmed boys or girls, finding the class a going concern, will come to it naturally, and the class will soon be an established institution. As I write I have before me the names of the ten boys who, when I came to this parish in 1911, promised to 'keep the flag flying till the newly confirmed join us.' The list includes the first lad killed from this parish in the war, and the last killed, just before the Armistice, and five others who gave their lives.

(v) It is impossible to leave the question of the management of boys without saying a word about serving at the altar as work for lads. I do not hesitate to say that in the last eighteen years it has been my most powerful weapon. Since getting out of bed is not easy for any boy, it makes some real calls on a boy's earnestness. As there are things to be done, and not merely talks to be listened to, serving supplies that expression for a lad's religious feelings which educationalists declare to be necessary when they say that there is 'no impression without expression.' As the position of a server is one which is both public and privileged, it makes a great call on a boy to try and live up to it, a call to which few if any boys are deaf. And, finally, it gives a lad an intelligent interest in, and understanding of, the highest form of worship. The best testimony to the value of having servers is that while there may be, just at first, some prejudice against them among the general congregation, there is never any on the part of their parents. Quite recently one woman said to me, 'I'm sure I've thanked God a score of times that you asked our John to serve. It's been the making of him,' and another said, 'All my boys have been on the altar, and if I had half a dozen more I'd like them all to follow the same way.' And these are but typical of scores of similar testimonies. Only take care that the serving is not monopolised by two or three boys. If it is, you will get just that type of gentle pious boy least in need of the help of a server's work, and whose serving is of little value as a witness to other lads. The ideal is that work as a server should be open to every steady, well-conducted boy about the church, and not simply to the ecclesiastically minded. In practice, it is of course impossible to find a place for all the boys. But spread your net as widely as possible. If you have only one celebration, an eight o'clock one, every Sunday, with one or two midday ones a month, and one weekday once each week, no boy should be allowed to serve more than once a month, which allows for nine or ten servers. Where there is a daily Eucharist and a choral celebration, with some little ceremonial, on Sundays room may easily be found for forty or fifty boys on the servers' roll. I am glad to say there are not a few families in both my last two parishes in which every boy has been a server.

Girls and Young Women

(i) So many of the things which I have said about boys are equally applicable to girls, that it is not necessary to write very fully about their management. But do not let it be said, 'The boys get everything in this parish. The girls are neglected.' Girls are easier to keep to church up to the time of their marriage than boys; but of those so kept a larger proportion lapse immediately after marriage. What I mean is, that a lad who can be kept steady to his church till he is five-and-twenty will generally, bar accidents, still keep to his church for life. Many a girl, a regular communicant and guild member up to her marriage, seems to drop all religion after marriage. In some cases there is real neglect of God, church and Sunday school having been mere social functions, opportunities for meeting friends and ultimately 'getting a young man.' But it is not always so. What seems neglect of religion is often due to the claims of home. We clergy would do well to recognise how much of a working woman's religion must and should display itself in care for the home. St. Paul knew it when he said of woman, 'She shall be saved in child-bearing.' For this reason it is very necessary to aim at giving our girls a strong *personal* religion, with power of prayer, habits of Bible reading, and love for God. The means are the same as in the case of the boy, namely, Bible Class, careful teaching at Confirmation, and monthly communicants' class with a written or printed notice. There is nothing for girls which takes the place of serving, but being much less shy and self-conscious than boys more use can be made of a guild, with its badge, monthly office, annual service and procession, and other features.

(ii) Obviously the curate, even if married and middle-aged, cannot work with girls in quite the same intimate and personal way as with boys. The Girls' Club, Girl Guides, Girls' Friendly Society, or other organisation must be under the direction of a lady. And her character is of supreme importance. I have known so many splendid lady workers, that I hesitate to say a word which may sound like harsh criticism. But some church workers are, I am sure, too lacking in humanity. I have known workers, male as well as female, who seemed to think it a crime for a girl to speak to a boy, and could never see a boy and girl over sixteen together without suspecting evil. That is a great mistake. The more boys and girls can be brought together, in a natural and healthy way and under good conditions, the better. Joint excursions of the senior members of the Lads' and Girls' Clubs, parish dances, and similar opportunities of meeting for young men and women are preventive of, rather than conducive to, evil. There is to-day a spirit of liberty abroad, which need not necessarily degenerate into license, and the Church will not lose, but gain, if she recognises that many things, such as fun, games, open air and exercise, and intellectual interests are as suitable and as necessary for girls as for boys. A girls' camp, for instance, while it cannot be run on quite such simple and rough lines as the lads' camp already described, is a valuable asset in the work of a parish. For some years now a lady connected with this parish has taken a cottage in the country near Manchester for a couple of months each summer. There ten or a dozen girls stayed week by week with her, doing their own work and cooking. A great feature was that each week the incoming party were brought to the cottage by their brothers, and the outgoing party fetched, so that Saturday afternoon each week was the occasion of a kind of picnic at the cottage.

Mothers

(i) I can perhaps best deal with work among the women of a parish by detailing the services and organisations I have found useful. First and foremost, I would put the 9.30 A.M. Eucharist every Monday. For many busy mothers of families, Sunday at 8 A.M. is a quite impossible hour, though where there is a 7 A.M. celebration every Sunday, as well as an eight o'clock one, many working women will come to it. A pleasant young mother of a growing family said to me the other day: 'The seven o'clock on a Sunday is just what I want. I really can't manage the other services, but my master never minds taking care of baby in bed of a Sunday morning, and it seems to begin the day well.' But where there is not a seven o'clock celebration, and often where there is, Sunday is impossible for many mothers. And in some homes Saturday night is no preparation. But Monday at 9.30 A.M. is just right. Sunday night has afforded an opportunity for preparation, the children are safe in school, the week's work has not begun, and all conditions are favourable. I have never known a man who tried a 9.30 A.M. celebration for mothers who did not confess its value. It is far better than 10 A.M. on Thursdays. Also in one parish it proved a valuable weapon in the fight against Monday morning drinking among women. And if the hints given in Chapter III. (p. 101) about the use of special intercessions are followed, the service is sure to be appreciated. Only it should be every Monday. Few women remember which is the first Monday in the month, and if for any reason a mother misses the monthly Communion, she may go two or three months without coming, and that tends to carelessness. Nor, if the service is desired as an opportunity of intercession for a sick child or a husband out of work, is there much point in waiting a month.

(ii) Along with the weekly Eucharist should go the afternoon service for women. A colleague of mine started one on Wednesday at three o'clock some years ago, and I am astonished at its success and at the way the women speak of it. The order is as follows :

Hymn, short prayers, hymn, address, hymn, Blessing. The addresses should not be casual sermons, but courses of instructions on the Prayer Book, the Creed, the Lord's Prayer, etc., and a printed syllabus is a good thing. There should not, I think, be a collection more often than monthly, but the members will welcome an opportunity, once a month, to give in support of some object that appeals to them, such as Rescue Work, the Mothers' Holiday Home, or mission work. The mothers' service need not compete with the usual Monday afternoon Mothers' Meeting.

(iii) The Mothers' Union is invaluable in a parish, and even if there are many other organisations and services in the parish it should not be neglected. A special quarterly or even annual celebration and a quarterly service is enough. Here the women's Wednesday service gives place once a quarter to the quarterly Mothers' Union service, the only difference being that the Mothers' Union office is said, and that after the service the members have tea together, for which they pay 6*d*. each, in the parish room, followed by an address from a lady speaker. By running the Wednesday service, which is open to all women, and the Mothers' Union, which is confined to communicants, thus together many mothers are led to think seriously of Confirmation.

(iv) Much good may be done by having a special service for mothers on the Monday (or Wednesday) in the Octave of the Purification, an invitation to which is sent to every mother who has had a child baptised during the previous year. The service should be followed, as in the case of the quarterly Mothers' Union service, by a tea in the parish room. For this special occasion, when comparative strangers are invited, the tea may well be free if the expense can be met. Such teas, giving the women a chance of friendly intercourse, have real value. For this same reason I value highly the annual picnic of the Mothers' Meeting, Mothers' Union, Women's Service, or other mothers' organisations.

(v) Manchester, and doubtless many other places, is fortunate enough to possess a Women's Holiday Home, where a working-class mother, with, if necessary, one small child, can spend a week at small charge. Much the best results from the Church point of view will be gained if arrangements can be made, well in advance, for the entire home to be reserved for one week for the mothers from a single parish. Then they are all friends together. If there is no such holiday home in a diocese, steps might well be taken to start one. Full details of the cost, management, and character of the Cathedral Holiday Home, Manchester, would, I am sure, be gladly supplied by the secretary to anyone wishing to start a similar home elsewhere.

Men

Work with men is so important and so difficult, and varies so much in different classes and districts, that I dare not attempt to treat it in detail here. But one thing I must say. All work with men should be actively and definitely religious. Many, very many, men will accept the advantages of a church club and yet keep religion at arm's length. Therefore, our chief aim should be to get to close grips with our men. The C.E.M.S. may be a most valuable agency in this work. It may, on the other hand, be completely useless. To make it an excuse for enrolling members whose church work is purely nominal and apparently limited to wearing a medal, and to allow it to become a mere agency for providing second-rate lectures and debates, is the road to ruin. The things men need are a regular communicants' class, a Bible study circle, a keen missionary guild, and a prayer-meeting at which the members go on their knees and pray in turn. All these things may spring from, and gather round, a strong C.E.M.S. branch.

explaining their nature and object, and giving the congregation an opportunity to express their views. I believe that there is nothing which has done so much harm to the Church of England, nothing which has so emptied churches and alienated the laity, as arbitrary changes made by newly appointed clergy—changes which the congregations have neither desired nor understood. The parish church is not the property of the clergyman, or the patron, or the whole Church, but of the people of the parish, and though, within certain well-defined limits, the hours of service and the character of the ceremonial are matters for the clergyman to decide, the clergy should always remember that they themselves are not 'lords over God's heritage' but 'ministers,' that is, servants of God's people. I have, unfortunately, seen much in the last thirty years of parishes where a High-Churchman has been appointed over an old-fashioned Low Church congregation, or where a Low-Churchman has been appointed to a church where the people have for years been accustomed to High Church teaching and practice, and I cannot protest too strongly against the cruelty and folly of such appointments. No one who has witnessed the fruit of such action at close quarters, and who knows the inevitable heart burnings and bitterness, the workers driven away, the old people made hard and quarrelsome, the young people sent adrift to indifference and irreligion, can think lightly of upsetting the traditions of a church and parish. I do not admit the right of any parson, nor of any patron, whether bishop, lay patron, or party society, to ride rough-shod over the wishes of a congregation. There are, of course, things which a man cannot conscientiously do. A High-Churchman may feel that he cannot conscientiously continue evening Communion; a Low-Churchman may feel that he cannot wear eucharistic vestments. But a man ought not, in such a case, to have accepted nomination to the parish.

There is one type of parish where drastic changes often seem allowable, and indeed called for. I mean the sort of parish where, owing to the long illness, great age, or bad character of the last incumbent, or for some other reason, the congregation has almost entirely vanished. A clergyman is often told in such cases, 'You'll have practically a free hand and will be able to do pretty well as you like, for there is only a mere remnant of the old congregation left.' Now, it is just in such a case that drastic changes and autocratic action on the part of the new incumbent seem to me at once most cruel and most impolitic. It is most cruel, for who are the people who compose this 'mere remnant'? They are a few faithful souls who have stuck to the church through thick and thin, never to be discouraged, always hoping for better times. Perhaps they have looked eagerly forward to the coming of the new incumbent, longing for sympathy, encouragement, and leadership. Why, after years of faithful work and patient waiting, should they find themselves slighted and ignored, and be driven from a church they have served so well? And as in such a case autocratic action on the part of a new incumbent is most cruel, so too it is most impolitic. There are sure to be many people who, if they no longer come to the church, yet count themselves as members of it, or at least have never settled anywhere else. These may easily be brought back to church. Only a few weeks ago I was hearing of the work of a man recently appointed to a church which for twelve or fifteen years has been a byword for neglect and desolation. My informant said, 'He's the right man, I can tell you. He's doing grand work. He's getting all the old families back again.' But these one-time worshippers are not likely to return if they hear that the few who stuck to the church in its worst time are discontented and angry. Indeed, it is only through, and by means of, the faithful remnant that such former members can be reached and regained.

Do I therefore mean that every new incumbent is to carry on the work of his parish exactly on the lines of his predecessor? By no means. As the work develops changes are inevitable, and no two men are likely to work in exactly the same way. But a congregation are far more likely to accept a man's teaching, and to fall in with his wishes, when they know and trust him than they are when he first arrives, and a conviction that he respects their feelings and is willing to consult them will do very much to disarm opposition. Indeed, where a congregation believes that the parson is a worker, with his whole heart in the success of his church, it is extraordinary how willing the people are to be guided by him. If, therefore, you want to make changes, wait till you have gained the confidence and affection of your people, and, above all, be willing to rule as a constitutional ruler with the consent of your Church Council. If this had always been the plan adopted, the progress of the revival which issued from the Oxford Movement might have been slower, though I am by no means sure of this, but it would certainly have been sounder, more uniform, and more fruitful.

I know that many people will disagree with what I have written. I have often heard it said, ' It's better to begin as you mean to go on. Get what you want straight away and then things have a chance to settle down. Nothing is worse policy than making two bites at a cherry.' Well, of course, if a man's ideal of the management of a parish is summed up in ' getting what he wants,' no doubt he may as well begin as he means to go on. But otherwise I am sure the policy of making changes before you have won the trust and confidence of the people is a bad one.

(ii) Quite apart from changes in ritual and ceremonial it is often possible, and indeed highly desirable, to make developments, for many churches are not put to anything like the best use. Nearly every church and parish has its special character which determines the use to be made of it. If the church is a central city church, past which thousands of people swarm all day, and the parish one which is all but deserted after 6 P.M., it is obviously little use having late evening services, but it may well be an ideal centre for midday addresses. If, on the other hand, the parish is what I have heard called a ' dormitory ' parish—one, that is to say, altogether inhabited by people who make their living elsewhere, as is the case with many South London parishes—then the church services, apart from services for children and for mothers, must be quite early in the day or else quite late. A city church near a big railway station may be made a place of rest and prayer for the poorer class of workers who have to come into town long before their places of business open in order to secure the concession of 'workman's fares.' The church of a well-to-do residential parish, where the majority of the parishioners dine late and do not like to come out after dinner, should have its services in the afternoon, though many educated men and women will make the effort, as a piece of self-denial, of coming out one night a week in Advent or Lent for a really good course of lectures or special sermons. If there are large mills or other works near a church, a short dinner-hour service once a week will be valued by many of the workers. I know one such church where, for the last ten years, a short Wednesday service, from 1.20 P.M. to 1.45 P.M., consisting of hymn, an eight minutes' address, eight minutes of prayer, hymn and Grace, has been always well attended. A church near a tram depôt should be the headquarters of the Tramway Workers' Guild; one near a big hospital, or in a neighbourhood where there are many nursing-homes, should be the centre for the Guild of St. Barnabas for Nurses. Much can be done at a church which is at the meeting point of many tram routes. Or, if there are many big hotels in the neighbourhood of a church, it is a good thing to have a list of the services printed on a good stout card with a loop of string to hang it by, and to ask the proprietor to hang a copy in each bedroom.

Many commercial travellers, and other people who have to spend much time in hotels, are very grateful for the information. The same is true of very many actors. But members of travelling companies, who are acting late on Saturday night and have to travel all Sunday, cannot attend ordinary Sunday services. If a church aims at being the centre for the Actors' Church Union, a 9.30 A.M. Monday celebration of Holy Communion is invaluable. One church that I know well does a great work with railway men, another with street-hawkers. All this, set down in bald record, may not seem very valuable. But my point is this, that every clergyman, looking at his new church and parish and estimating its possibilities, should ask what he can do to make full use of his church over and above the ordinary parochial activities. Some clergy, and even I fear some wardens, are inclined to regard such extra-parochial efforts as waste of time, and to declare that they 'bring nobody to the ordinary services of the church.' If this were true, I should not think it mattered, since it is just the soul which can't, or won't, come to the ordinary services of the church which the clergyman is most bound to 'go after . . . until he find it.' But I am sure it is false. Many years ago I knew two central city churches. One was allowed to fall into neglect and torpor, with the result that it was pulled down and the site sold, though tens of thousands passed its doors daily, and opposite the site, which is now an open space, there now stands one of the biggest hotels in the country, the permanent staff of which would alone have afforded a clergyman

P

with any initiative adequate work, and the visitors to which offer a boundless field for effort. The other church, though undoubtedly well placed, was distinctly less so than the one pulled down. But the rector has made it the centre of one of the most remarkable series of Advent and Lent midday addresses in England—a series which has now been running, unbroken, for something like twenty years. The result has not merely been to benefit the church life of the whole city, but so to keep alive the spirit of the place that its Sunday services are probably better attended than those in any city church of its kind.

(iii) In connection with the ideas suggested by the last paragraph there are two cautions I would offer which, if duly laid to heart, may prove valuable. I will venture to express them in antinomy:

(*a*) The fact that any particular course of action has proved successful in another parish is fair proof that it will be successful in yours.

(*b*) The fact that any particular course of action has proved successful in another parish is no proof that it will be successful in yours.

The first caution is perhaps the most necessary, because the least obvious. Often and often when, on a mission or on some similar occasion, I have advised some course of action, I've been met with the objection: 'I'm sure it's a splendid idea, and no doubt it would work well in many parishes. But I'm afraid it would be no use trying it here. Our people are very funny; they are not like most people, etc., etc.' Now all this is rubbish pure and undiluted. It is not in the least likely that six or eight thousand people in one parish are any more or less funny than an equal number of people in any other parish, and the excuse springs from laziness, timidity, and lack of initiative. Human nature, broadly speaking, is the same everywhere.

One is bound to admit, on the other hand, that a thing which is well suited to one parish may be quite unsuited to another. I knew a man who went from a large well-appointed parish church, where there were well-to-do and educated people with plenty of leisure, to a small working-class parish in a 'cotton' town, where every person not needed for housework or the care of the children went into the mill at 6 A.M. Yet he tried to reproduce everything he had been accustomed to at the first church, from the 8 A.M. daily Eucharist to the afternoon devotional services in Lent. And when no one came (there was no one who could come) he decided that his people were very funny people and did not respond to sacramental teaching or desire opportunities of worship. If it is true that human nature, broadly speaking, is the same everywhere, it is equally true that local conditions are, broadly speaking, different everywhere. And even where local conditions are alike, it is well to remember that the people of a parish which has been well worked for years are more likely to respond to special efforts than one where nothing has been done beyond the minimum of obligatory services for a long time. If a man will study the character and needs of his people carefully, use common sense, and set his heart on making the very most of his opportunities, he will very soon see the results of his efforts.

(iv) I have spent enough (some readers may be inclined to say too much) time on the discussion of general principles. Let us now ask what should be the first task of a new incumbent. Unless his predecessor has left him one, I have no hesitation in saying that his first task should be the compiling of a full and accurate list of the names and addresses of all communicants. It is absolutely impossible to work a parish unless you have the names and addresses of your people. And if such names and addresses have to be sought in half a dozen different registers, it trebles work and makes it almost impossible to avoid missing some. It is best therefore, directly you come to a church, to ask that everyone will fill up, and place in a box in church, a slip giving full name and address. Explain the matter from the pulpit, telling the people that the fact that anyone has been 'attending this church for twenty years' does not help a newly arrived stranger, who during those twenty years was in another part of England, to know his or her name and address. Remind them that what is wanted is a good list of names and addresses, and that when the parson sits down to write out such a list, it is much easier for him if he has only to copy from a number of slips of paper than if he has to try and remember some scores, perhaps hundreds of people whom he has met once in church, in the day or Sunday schools, at another person's house, or in the street. Point out how little use a paper is if it contains nothing but the words 'C. L. Smith,

King Street,' which may refer to Mr., Mrs., Master, or Miss Charles Lawrence, or Clara Lilian, Smith in any one of perhaps five or six King Streets, and how helpful a list is which reads :

Henry Smith (Mr.) Elizabeth Smith (Mrs.) George Smith (20 yrs.) Alice Smith (18 yrs.) Grace Smith (15 yrs.) William Smith (14 yrs.)	All confirmed.
Mary Smith (12 yrs.) Cyril Smith (9 yrs.)	Not confirmed.

Jane Brown, servant, a communicant.
13 King Street, Pendleton.

Of course, no amount of talking will induce everyone to take the trouble to fill in a slip. Some don't because they come to church so often you ought to know them. Some don't because they come so seldom it didn't seem worth while. Some don't because they thought some one else would be sure to tell you about them, though it never crossed their minds themselves to tell you about anyone else. And, needless to say, it is just the people who won't take the trouble to let you know of their existence who will be most indignant with you for not calling. But a well-posted list of names and addresses is an absolute necessity if a parish is to be properly worked, and I know of no other way of getting one started.

It is a very good thing, where it can be managed, to have all attendances at Holy Communion entered, using the communicants' roll not only as a list of names and addresses, but also as a register of attendances. For it is extraordinarily difficult, unless such a record is kept, to tell who is and who is not lapsing from Communion. A mere vague impression that you have not seen some particular person at Communion for some weeks is hardly sufficient ground for a pastoral visit and an inquiry on the point. On the other hand, if some girl or young man does not come to Communion for months, perhaps out of mere carelessness or forgetfulness at first, and nothing is said by the parish priest, it cannot be wondered at if the offender thinks it does not matter. I used to think it might annoy and offend people for the clergyman to call and say, 'I have not seen you at Communion for such and such a time.' I know now that, so far from being offended, they are almost always grateful and pleased. They feel that they have been missed, and that they are valued. The best way is to get some regular attender to write down the names of those present each Sunday. If such a person comes early, so as to say her own preparatory prayers before others begin to come in, she can write down the names of others before the service without disturbing her own devotions, and can check her list, and add the names of late comers, as the congregation leaves church. It is not easy to get anyone who will know everyone who attends, and it may be well to have a lady to make a list of all women and girls, and a man to make one of the men and boys. The lady who for many years did the work for me used to give me a list of all the women and girls, and give also the number of men and boys present. I used to check this against my recollection of the men and boys who were present—it being much easier for the clergyman to remember the men and boys, owing to their faces not being hid by hats as they kneel at the altar rails—and so few names were ever missed. I am sure this is a better plan than issuing to all members of the Communicants' Guild small cardboard slips to be put into a box in church, both because the latter plan introduces the idea of 'getting one's mark for being present' which, harmless in connection with a Bible Class, is not quite in place in connection with the Blessed Sacrament, and also because the object of keeping a record is chiefly to note the presence or absence of just those persons who are least likely to be members of a guild. A well-kept record should show the attendances of all communicants, and should help the parson not to overlook any strangers who may attend his church. It is abundantly worth the trouble, as anyone will admit who has tried it.

(v) When there is a good list of names and addresses of all communicants, the next step is to get a good church council into working order, if such a thing does not already exist. It cannot be denied that many churchwardens are even more hostile to church councils than some clergy. They are frequently busy men. They have little time to spare for what they regard as needless discussion, and if they have been long in office they often resent having the undisputed control of affairs taken out of their hands by a number of younger men who, they say, have no real responsibility if things go badly. This is a situation which needs tact. It is easy to offend staid, useful, and capable men, and then to find the most noisy and talkative members of the church council the least ready to do any real work, and perhaps all the members very inclined to grow slack when the first novelty has worn off. Yet all schemes of church reform build, and as I think rightly build, on the church council, and no good will be done in the Church of England, I am sure, without a great extension of democratic control. The autocracy of wardens, especially if it is supposed that they are chosen because of their wealth or social position, can be even more harmful to a church than the autocracy of the parson. The best way of dealing with the matter is by giving the church council real power in return for its acceptance of real financial responsibility. Small sub-committees, with or without power to co-opt outsiders, for the management of different organisations, are a good thing. And slackness of attendance, which is often due to there not being any very urgent or interesting business to do when the council does meet, may be cured by having all business and questions for discussion at the monthly meeting sent to the secretary at least a fortnight in advance. Then if there is nothing which calls for a meeting, no meeting need be held. But it is well to make a rule that not more than two meetings in succession shall be dropped, so that the council will always meet at least once a quarter. In a really well-worked parish, where things are being vigorously pushed forward, it should not be necessary to drop any monthly meetings, except perhaps in the middle of summer.

(vi) One matter should engage the early and careful attention of the parson, and that is the finance of the parish. The hand-to-mouth methods of many poor parishes are at once expensive and ineffectual. The fabric of the church is allowed to get out of repair, the inside is dirty, the books, alike for the choir and for loan to strangers, are ragged and imperfect, the altar linen and surplices need renewal, and a score of small things need doing for which there are no funds. Add to this that the salaries of all who work for the church—incumbent, curate, lay reader, lady worker, organist, caretaker, and cleaner—are on the lowest possible scale, and lay the church open to the charge of 'sweating,' and it will be seen how important the subject of finance is. Many churches depend on periodical efforts of a special kind, such as an annual sale of work, concert, or other way of raising money. I do not wish to condemn such things. Properly managed they can do much good, even if, improperly managed, they do great harm. But the ideal of the Church should undoubtedly be *an adequate income of a fairly regular amount supplied by the free-will offerings of the people.* Much has been written on the subject, and I do not propose here to discuss the question of parish finance in detail. But one point I would lay stress on. The whole financial burden of a church should not rest on the shoulders of a comparatively small number of regular and faithful attenders, but should be distributed, as far as possible, over the whole lot of those who, while not coming to church regularly, and so contributing little or nothing to the collections, nevertheless consider themselves members of the church, and use it for baptisms, marriages, and funerals, send their children to the day and Sunday schools, and call for the ministrations of the clergy in times of sickness. A large proportion of such people are, as I have proved by experience, quite willing to recognise their responsibilities, and to contribute to the support of the church, if the matter is brought before them in the right way. In my present parish this is accomplished by means of regular weekly collections, made from house to house, by ladies, each of whom is responsible for from ten to fifty houses. When the Manchester Diocesan Church Levy Fund was first started, some seven years ago, the parish was assessed at a sum which it seemed quite beyond our power to raise. But a meeting was held, and after much discussion a plan was arranged. Every house in the parish was visited, and a letter left at each which set forth the needs of the church, the responsibility of the people, and the ease with which the money might be raised if all members of the Church of England would promise small sums of from *2d.* to 1*s.* weekly. Such sums, it was explained, would be called for. Quite half the population of the parish is Roman Catholic, and it also contains a large and well-worked Wesleyan mission. Yet quite a surprisingly large number of people promised to give weekly sums. The result has been that not merely has the church succeeded in paying its full quota to the levy every year, but there has always been a substantial sum over for general purposes. Indeed, the amount that can be collected seems only limited by the number of persons willing to act as collectors. Many ladies shrink from undertaking the work, but all who have tried it declare that it is one of the pleasantest forms of parochial visiting, displaying the people visited at their best, as indeed is quite likely, since 'it is more blessed to give than to receive,' and so the people welcome their collecting lady.

This plan seems to me better than the envelope scheme, in that it throws the burden on all who have any feeling of goodwill to the Church, and not only on those who come to the services as the envelope scheme tends to do. I dwell on this point because I know that in a poor parish the burden on those who do come to church is often a heavy one. Some years ago, before the war, a very zealous churchman, a member of a family all of whom were church workers, spoke to me strongly on the matter. He said that the expense of church-going was really a serious matter. There was something for the collection, for each member of a large family, twice each Sunday and three times on Communion Sunday. There was a subscription to this and a subscription to that, and tickets to be bought nearly every week for a concert, a party, a dance, or some other special effort. His wife was asked to give a cake for this sale, or to work something for that bazaar. And as soon as the funds of one society were put right, another, he declared, was always found to be in debt. There is, I am sure, much truth in this complaint. Hence it is well to 'broaden the basis of taxation,' as a statesman would say.

(vii) When what I may call the foundation of

parish work has been well and truly laid, when, that is to say, the communicants' roll has been formed and names of new members of the church, or of old members returned to it, are being constantly added to it, when the church council has been formed and is working well, and when the church levy collectors are calling regularly and bringing in sums, small perhaps individually but large in the aggregate, the parson should look round for ways of stimulating interest, rousing enthusiasm, and deepening devotion. What I complain of in the management of many parishes, is that it lacks initiative, imagination, and originality. I have nothing to say against what is called quiet pastoral work. Indeed, the whole of this book is inspired by the conviction that it is the thing most vital to the life of the Church. But quiet pastoral work should not be allowed to degenerate into sleepy pastoral work. Times of refreshing and revival are of value to all of us if they are calls to renewed devotion, and not mere appeals to excited emotion. I want therefore to discuss some methods of stimulating interest and devotion. Some will be of such a nature that they can be, and should be, repeated at regular intervals. Some will be, by their very nature, exceptional. Foremost among the first class I would mention the putting out of the Lent and Advent papers. Our Prayer Book clearly contemplates a definite use of the Church's seasons, her feasts and fasts, as a means of teaching and training our people, and many churches still, I fancy, fail to make full use of this opportunity. The Advent or Lent paper should not be a mere handbill giving a list of preachers and services. Still less should it be sent out with blanks upon it, and notices such as 'Preacher to be announced later.' Such an announcement merely advertises the fact that the clergyman has left making his arrangements too late. Let the Advent or Lent paper be at least a four-page leaflet—in large parishes where there is a district church or mission it may easily swell into a small booklet—with a pastoral letter, on the front page, from the pastor to the faithful. Then follow the details of Sunday services, special week-day courses, hours of Communion, arrangements for the children's services, open-air services, parochial quiet day, and services in preparation for the Christmas or Easter Communion. At the top of the front page should be printed, in large type: 'Please put this up in your house where all members of the household can see it.' The paper may either be left at all houses in the parish, as explained in Chapter II, or sent by post to each household on the communicants' roll, which is an excellent way of checking the extent to which it is up to date, or merely given out as people leave church, which last I hold to be the least valuable way. The expense need be no difficulty, since the people may be asked either to put a penny in a special box in church, or to give a little extra at a special collection, in either of which cases a good deal more than the cost of the paper is sure to be received.

(viii) In parishes where confessions are heard—and I have already given my reasons for thinking that they should be heard in all parishes where the Prayer Book is accepted as a guide to loyal church people—the question will rise whether notice should be given of regular times when the clergy will be in church to hear them. The reasons usually given against printing such notices are two—first, that many people who do not use confession will be alarmed and offended; and second, that where not many people come it is more convenient, and a saving of time, to let penitents make appointments at times that suit them. I am sure both arguments are wrong. No man has less desire than I to force confession on those who do not desire it. I regard it as a medicine, not a food, and though I am sure that many people would benefit greatly by using it who do not do so, yet I recognise that, whether as a matter of loyalty to the Prayer Book, which leaves it optional, or whether as a matter of policy, people who need it being more likely to come if not unduly urged, the parson should not try to press it upon his flock. But I am sure that nothing has done so much harm as making a mystery about confession. If confessions are heard, let it be at fixed times, and in the open church, and let there be no concealment or mystery. And as to the argument about convenience and waste of time, I think the real weight of the argument is on the other side. Less time is wasted in having a fixed hour two or three days a week than in making a number of special appointments at various times for different people. And if no one comes a quiet hour in church need never be wasted, for it affords a valuable time, to an overworked priest, when he can prepare a sermon, make a meditation, pray, or read a devotional book. As this book claims to be based on experience, I would record that the first time I put the times for confessions on my Lent paper I explained in the accompanying pastoral letter that my doing so marked no change in my teaching or practice, and that I had no desire to press the use of confession on any who did not desire to use it. The results were threefold: (1) No one was in the least offended or disturbed; (2) many people came, including some total strangers, who had never been to me before, showing that some people shrink from making appointments, or at least that fixed times were convenient to them; (3) I was spared the trouble of writing many letters, and on the rare occasions when no one came I found the hour of perfect quiet a great refreshment, and a really valuable opportunity for prayer and thought. So I would strongly advise putting a notice of the times for confession on the Advent and Lent papers. Such times should include at least one hour a week in the evening for working people, and one in the afternoon for those who do not go out to work during the day. An hour, on one other day, in the morning is a convenience to clergy and nurses on night work and some other classes. Obviously more numerous opportunities should be given in Holy Week and the week just before Christmas.

(ix) I have written above of a Parochial Quiet Day as one of the things of which a Lent or Advent paper may give notice. I ought perhaps to have written Quiet Afternoon, for few parishes, at any rate of the type with which I am familiar, could manage a whole day. But a Quiet Afternoon is a very valuable thing in any well-worked parish. A celebration, or perhaps two, at convenient hours in the morning for those who propose to attend the Quiet Afternoon, and then something like the following programme—

3.30 P.M. Devotions and first address.
4.30 P.M. Devotions and second address.
5.30 P.M. Tea in the parish room.
6.30 P.M. Evensong and third address.

will be found to work well. But let the devotions and addresses be of such a length as will leave adequate time for silence—many Quiet Afternoons seem to be so named on the *lucus à non lucendo* principle because some one is talking the whole time—and let those who attend feel quite free, between the sessions, to kneel, sit, or walk in the churchyard as they please. Those who want tea should be asked to send in their names beforehand. The Quiet Afternoon may sometimes be announced as one 'for Missions,' the addresses being on missionary subjects, and a missionary biography being read at tea.

(x) If the conditions of the parish are such as to suit, nothing is more helpful in evangelistic work, or more beneficial to those of the church who can be induced to take part, than open-air processions and open-air preaching. I distinguish between processions and preaching because there is a great difference in the way things should be managed where the procession, the mere marching through the streets that is to say, is the object of going out, and where on the other hand the preaching is the chief thing, and the clergy, choir, and congregation merely pass from one station to the other. In the first case, everything should be done to make the procession striking and effective, the congregation should be urged to march four abreast, and should be marshalled by men carrying wands of office, the church officers with their staves should head the procession, and if it is dark there should be plenty of lantern bearers carrying large 'guard' lanterns on sticks. For eight or nine years in succession in my last parish the whole congregation turned out every Wednesday night at 8.30 P.M., after the 7.30 Evensong and sermon, and walked round the parish headed by the clergy and choir, and accompanied by plenty of lantern bearers, singing hymns to the accompaniment of cornets, the object being to draw in a congregation for a 9 P.M. lantern service in church. I fear lantern services for adults, and even for children, have largely had their day, the cinematograph having killed them. But a well-ordered procession, with its white-robed choir, gleaming lights, and sounding cornets is very effective in dark back streets, and is still very useful for drawing in a congregation for a simple mission service. And it is an excellent thing for the laity thus to witness publicly, in the open street, to their service of Christ.

A similarly striking and well-ordered procession is useful for open-air preaching after Evensong on Sunday, during the summer months, or on Good Friday, say from 5 P.M. to 6.30 P.M. But where such a procession cannot, for any reason, be managed, the open-air preaching, if the conditions of the parish are such as to call for it, ought not to be omitted. Some of the most fruitful open-air preaching I ever knew was done by a clergyman who used to march out, on a Sunday evening, into a big East End thoroughfare, attired in his cassock and carrying a chair. The chair he planted at a street corner, and having sung a hymn, giving out hymn papers as he did so to any who gathered round, he used to mount a chair and preach. When I first came to the parish one of the most devout communicants was a one-time Unitarian woman converted by this preaching. But we have not all got this man's courage. But wherever a small knot of faithful people can be persuaded to volunteer to act as choir, distributors of hymn papers, and (if the expression is allowable) decoy congregation, there the parson should try open-air preaching. A cornet, if well played, is far the best instrument for leading the hymns, but a small portable harmonium is excellent, and a concertina, as both the Salvation Army and Church Army know well, is very useful. In a parish of well-to-do gentlefolk who would almost as soon think of going to bed in the public streets as of listening to a preacher at the street corner, open-air preaching is doubtless out of place. Everywhere else, I am sure, it is infinitely valuable, whether done in the simplest way by a few enthusiasts, or in the most striking and dignified way with surpliced choir, banners, music, and marshals. Many clergy tell me open-air preaching does no good. Secularists, socialists, suffragists, and politicians of all parties know better. I need scarcely add that lay preachers are specially valuable in the open air. Objectors can't say of a keen layman, 'Eh, he's paid for it.'

(xi) One type of open-air procession I have tried with really amazing results. I had long been anxious to revive the old custom of the Rogation-tide procession, but the occasion did not seem to offer. Then, some ten or twelve years ago, we had in Manchester eighteen months or two years of unexampled depression of trade and consequent poverty. Here was the opportunity to impress on the people the value of prayer, and in so doing to revive the observance of Rogation-tide. The ideal plan would have been an early morning procession round the parish, with a return to church for a parochial Eucharist. But the ideal plan is not always the most practically useful. An extremely early hour, certainly not later than 4.30 A.M., would have been necessary if many of our people were to take part in the procession, be present at the celebration, and get away in time for work. Such an hour would not merely be difficult for all, impossible for some, and dangerous for many growing girls and boys with a long day's work before them, but would have the further disadvantage that the streets would be empty of all except those taking part, and the effect would therefore be lost. It is also a question, and a very grave one, how far, in the present state of religion in England, it is desirable to draw in large mixed congregations of casual strangers to celebrations of the Holy Communion. It was therefore decided that the congregation should assemble each day at 7.30 P.M. in church for a very brief service, lasting about ten minutes, and then go out in procession. On the first of the three Rogation Days the Bishop of Manchester walked with us, on the second the Archdeacon of Manchester, and on the third the Dean of Manchester. The church officers entered into the scheme with enthusiasm, and marched each night at the head bearing their staves of office. After them came the clergy, the choir, a small band, and the congregation marching four and four, and marshalled by about forty marshals carrying white wands of office. I do not think there were ever less than 500 walking, and on the last night the papers estimated the number at between 700 and 800. As the procession moved from station to station, a metrical litany, and hymn 142 A. and M. were sung. At each station a short psalm was sung, led by the choir-master on a concertina, a short address was given, and special prayers were offered. The stations were made at the doors of a big iron works, before the gates of a large railway goods yard, outside a great block of workman's dwellings, and at the doors of the church, the subjects of prayer being a revival of trade in Manchester, a revival of commerce throughout England, a blessing on the home life of our land, and a revival of religion among us. The hymns, psalms, and prayers were printed on a paper which also gave clear directions to the people as to marching, halting, joining in the services, and so on. Needless to say, the whole thing required careful thinking out and organising beforehand, and frequent meetings were held to enlist the interest, sympathy, and co-operation of the congregation, and especially of the men, without whose enthusiastic support nothing would have been accomplished. Only a few days before this paragraph was written a man, who had taken a leading part in the effort, said to me: 'I often look back to our first Rogation-tide processions. After their wonderful success all we young fellows felt there was nothing we could attempt at church which would not be a success if we went about it in the spirit of prayer and of faith. It was a revelation to all of us.' I have gone into this matter somewhat fully, for I believe there are times when something striking, spectacular, and novel is really helpful, and indeed necessary, for the spiritual life of a parish.

Our effort was a special one to meet special needs, and I did not therefore attempt to make it an annual affair. But I believe that in rural parishes, and on slightly modified lines, the Rogation-tide procession might become a valuable feature of parish life.

(xii) A less spectacular, but not less valuable, opportunity is offered by the Ember Days, and there is a special use of them, the value of which I have proved four or five times. When a new curate is expected, and even more when a young man who has been working in the parish as a layman is to be ordained deacon, or a deacon on the staff is to be ordained priest, a whole day of prayer should be held on one of the Ember Days, Saturday for preference. The day should begin with celebrations of Holy Communion at convenient hours, say one at 6 A.M. for early workers, one at 7.30 A.M. or 8 A.M. for ordinary people, and one at 9.30 A.M. for mothers. If a children's Eucharist is the custom of the parish, the 9.30 A.M. celebration may well be choral, as the elder school children will take the greatest interest in the idea of praying for their new pastor. All through the day there should be such special services as are likely to suit the people, such as a short dinner-hour service at 1 P.M., devotional service and address at 4.30 P.M., and Evensong and sermon at 7.30 P.M. The great thing to be aimed at is, however, not so much the services as the hours between. These should be divided into periods of a quarter of an hour or twenty minutes each, and a list of these times posted in the church some time before, with a request that members of the congregation should put their initials against those times when they can promise to be in church. The idea is that from the time the church opens for the first celebration till it closes at 10 P.M. there should always be somebody in church praying. Here and there odd quarters of an hour, awkward for ordinary people, may have to be undertaken by members of the staff, but if the idea is well explained to the people, and they are asked not to be slack in 'helping together by prayer for us, that for the gift bestowed upon us by the means of many persons thanks may be given by many' (2 Cor. i. 11), the response is sure to be a good one. The last time I tried it, the attendance at the early celebrations of Holy Communion was the best ever known on a weekday in the parish, there were never less than half a dozen, and often thirty or forty, persons praying silently in church, and, what was perhaps the most gratifying thing of all, a very large number of the lads and girls from the clubs came in between 9 P.M. and 10 P.M. for silent prayer, and stopped for the short closing service—just a few words of explanation of the object of the day of prayer and of the way it had been used, a hymn, a few collects, and the Grace—with which the day ended at 10 P.M.

One thing it is well to remember. Many people

find it very difficult to pray for any length of time without help. A number of printed or cyclostyled papers should therefore be placed in the seats suggesting suitable collects, hymns, and passages of Scripture for use as helps to prayer and meditation. Thus the paper may read:

The following collects will be found helpful:

(*a*) As a preparation for prayer: First Sunday after Epiphany. Septuagesima, 1st, 10th, 12th, 19th, and 23rd Sundays after Trinity.

(*b*) For the clergy: Collects for the Ember Weeks (to be found among the 'Prayers and Thanksgivings for Several Occasions,' which come just after the Litany in the Prayer Book) and Collects for 3rd Sunday in Advent, St. Matthias's Day, St. Peter's Day.

(*c*) For the Church and congregation: Collects for 5th, 15th, and 16th Sundays after Trinity, and for St. Bartholomew's Day, St. Luke's Day, and Sts. Simon and Jude.

The following hymns (*A. and M.*) *may be used as prayers:* 156, 157, 209, 353, 354, 355, 356, 363, 364, 470, and any others you may specially love.

The following passages of Holy Scripture may be read and prayed over:

The call of Abraham to God's service (Genesis xii. 1–3); Jacob's night of prayer (Genesis xxxii. 24–30); the power of intercessory prayer (Exodus xvii. 8–12); the gift of the Holy Spirit (Numbers xi. 24–29); the ordination of Joshua (Numbers xxvii. 18–23); the righteous and unrighteous priests (Samuel iii. 1–21); the vision of Isaiah and his call to service (Isaiah vi. 1–8); the Man of God and his message (Jeremiah xx. 7–9); the clergyman's duty (Ezekiel iii. 16–21); Christ's invitation to quiet and prayer (Mark vi. 31); Christ's prayer before calling His apostles (Luke vi. 12–13); the pattern for every pastor (John x. 11–14); the coming of the Holy Spirit (Acts ii. 1–4); the life of a missionary priest (2 Cor. vi. 1–10).

N.B.—The service for the ordination of a deacon or a priest may also be read and prayed over, especially the questions and exhortations addressed by the bishop to the candidates for Holy Orders. The service will be found at the end of your Prayer Book.

Unless some such help is provided, many people will come to pray and then find the time hang heavy on their hands. In that case some will leave with a feeling of disappointment and disillusionment. It is not a bad thing to print, in large type, on such a prayer paper: *Take this paper away with you and use it from time to time, especially at the four Ember seasons, in your own home.* This will help to a fruitful use of Ember-tide among the faithful of a parish. It is much to be feared that for many, even among fairly instructed church people, Ember-tide at present is a dead letter.

(xiii) I cannot omit, when treating of the various ways in which the spiritual life of a parish may be stimulated and deepened, to say something of parochial missions. But before I touch that subject I want to describe a modified form of teaching mission which I have found very useful, and which any parish priest should find himself well able to conduct. The qualities necessary for a missioner capable of conducting an evangelistic mission are not perhaps given to every man, though I am sure such qualities are much commoner than are supposed, and might be developed, to the great benefit of the Church, by many men if proper efforts were made in every diocese to discover, train, and use such gifts. But every preacher should be able to make himself a teacher, if he is willing to take sufficient pains. And since plain dogmatic teaching in the elements of the faith is one of the things most needed by the laity, teaching missions are of great value. Now there is one form of teaching mission which never fails to prove attractive. I owe the idea to Archdeacon Wakeford of Lincoln, who made great use of it when vicar of St. Margaret's, Anfield, Liverpool. I do not think he will mind my describing it here, nor charge me with infringing his patent. It is called a Parochial Convention, and consists of a series of services, usually six in number, and held once a week. At the first service each person who attends is given a coloured card, about 10 inches by 8 inches, on which is printed the outline of a cross:

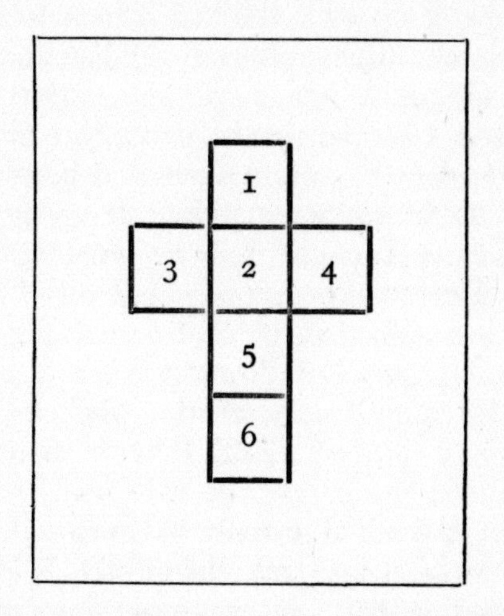

It will be seen that this cross is composed of six equal squares. At each service each person present is given a small square of paper, gummed at the back, on which is printed brief notes of the subject for the day. The convention service consists of a hymn, three collects, a second hymn, during the singing of which the ' stickies,' or small squares of paper, for the day are distributed by helpers, a lecture of about five-and-twenty or thirty minutes, a closing hymn, and the Blessing. What is wanted is not hortatory sermons but plain simple lectures, and great care must be taken to follow the line of thought set out in the printed notes which the people have in their hands during each lecture. When all six stickies are stuck on the card the cross is completed, and the card remains not merely a valued memento, but a constant reminder of the teaching given. I have seen our cards hung up over the bed in a score of houses. The idea seems simple and even childish, but what has surprised me most has been the enthusiasm with which it has been received by really educated men and women, doctors and bankers and hospital nurses, and teachers in elementary and secondary schools. Though indeed I ought not to have felt surprise. A parochial convention supplies not merely dogmatic teaching, but coherent dogmatic teaching in which the connection of one doctrine with another, and so the unity and beauty of the whole of Christian teaching, is displayed. And that is what all the laity, educated and simple, most desire.

My first parochial convention was a Convention on Christian Doctrine and, the church being a small one and seating only 560 persons, there were three sessions a week, one at 3 P.M. on Mondays for mothers and others who did not go out to business, one at 8 P.M. on Mondays for women and girls at business during the day, and one at 8.30 P.M. on Fridays for men and boys. By the end of the second week we had issued over 880 cards, and had to refuse to issue any more. And the curate in charge of the roll reported that less than 5 per cent. failed to 'complete their cross.' For it is a good thing to mark a roll. Let each card be numbered on the back, and as each is given out enter the number and the name and address of the recipient in a book. This takes a little time at the first service, but afterwards each person, on entering, simply gives the number of his or her card, which can be quickly written down on a piece of paper, and the register entered up afterwards at one's leisure. By this means many persons, brought to the convention by friends, or attracted by hearsay, can be visited and secured permanently. I print below the notes of my first Convention on Christian Doctrine, not because they are the best that could be produced, for they could easily be improved on, but as an illustration of what has been done.

I.

GOD *Manifested* (1) In experience.
(2) In the lives of the Saints.
(3) In the course of History.
(4) In the facts of Science.

GOD is *Spirit* (a) Almighty, (e) Eternal,
(i) Infinite, (o) One,
(u) Uncreated.

GOD is *Love,* in Creation.
in Redemption.
in Sanctification.

GOD, FATHER, SON, and HOLY GHOST.
Practical Outcome—Worship.

2. MAN IS A THREEFOLD BEING—

His Nature: (1) Body, (2) Mind, (3) Soul.

	(1)	(2)	(3)
His Needs:	Food and Exercise.	Ideas and Training.	Grace and Religion.
His Powers:	He can Know.	Can Love.	Can Choose.

His Faith shows itself in:
(1) Knowing God as his Creator.
(2) Loving God as his Father.
(3) Choosing God as his Master.

He was created:
(1) For God's glory.
(2) For his neighbour's service.
(3) For his own happiness.

He is a Fallen creature.	His Nature is corrupt.	His world is evil.

Practical Outcome—He needs Redemption.

3. JESUS: GOD-SAVIOUR.

TRUE GOD; able to save.

'No man can save his brother's soul.'

TRUE MAN; able to sympathise.

'In all points tempted like as we are.'

GRACE = CHRIST'S HUMAN NATURE:

(*a*) Human. (*c*) Complete. (*e*) Strengthened.
(*b*) Sinless. (*d*) Sanctified. (*f*) Enriched.

TERMS OF FORGIVENESS:

(i.) Hate sin. (ii.) Give in. (iii.) Feel pain.

JESUS CHRIST
Was all I ought to be;
Did all I ought to do;
Earned all I want to have.

4. GOD THE SON.

In the beginning.
- (i.) Image of the Father.
- (ii.) Word and Wisdom of God.
- (iii.) Pattern of Creation.

Since the Ascension.
- (i.) First Man in Heaven.
- (ii.) Our Representative.
- (iii.) Sender of the Comforter.

He works *for* us Himself in Heaven.
He works *in* us by His Spirit on Earth.

PROPHET. PRIEST. KING.

His Body is the Church.

Practical Outcome—The Sacraments.

5. GOD THE HOLY GHOST.

God's Agent.
- (i.) In Creation.
- (ii.) In the Incarnation.
- (iii.) In the New Creation.

Spirit of
- (*a*) Regeneration.
- (*b*) Conversion.
- (*c*) Justification.
- (*d*) Confirmation.
- (*e*) Sanctification.

He takes of the things of Christ.
He distributes to every man as He will.

Practical Outcome—Conversion.

6. THE CHURCH UNIVERSAL.

(1) A Divine Society:

'A city set on a hill.'

(2) The Body of Christ:

'Ye are the Body of Christ.

{ Admission to this Society by Baptism.
{ Government of this Society by the Holy Spirit.

{ The Head of this Body is Christ.
{ The Nature of this Body is different organs for different work.

Marks of the Church: { (1) One. (3) Catholic.
{ (2) Holy. (4) Apostolic.

Her work: (i.) Conversion; (ii.) Edification.

N.B.—Doctrine and Jurisdiction.

Practical Outcome—Church Membership.

Where it is difficult to get the people together on a week night in any numbers, I have held the convention on the Sunday evenings in Lent, slightly shortening the service by having the psalms said and the canticles sung to simple chants, giving out the 'stickies' during the hymn after the Grace and letting the convention address take the place of the sermon. This, too, proved very successful. A 'Convention on Christian Doctrine' may be followed, the next year, by a 'Convention on the Devotional Life,' when the subjects may be:

(1) The Doctrine and Practice of Prayer.
(2) Personal and Intercessory Prayer.
(3) Bible Study and Meditation.
(4) The Use of the Sacraments.
(5) Public Worship.
(6) Christian Warfare in the World.

If it is objected that each one of these topics is wide enough to supply matter for a course of sermons, I would remind the objector that the object of a convention is not to give detailed teaching on any one doctrine or practice of Christianity, but to sketch, in broadest outline, the whole field of doctrine or of practice, thus both giving a bird's-eye view, which is so helpful to a beginner, and preparing the way for the detailed treatment of individual points of difficulty. It does not do to work the convention idea to death, and when a parochial convention has been held two, or at most three years running, it should be discontinued for some years.

(xiv) From a parochial convention or teaching mission one turns naturally to the thought of a real evangelistic mission conducted by missioners brought in from outside. This is too big a subject for treatment in a single paragraph, and there are besides several admirable books on the subject. But there are one or two points I wish to touch on. The first caution I would give is, Never, under any circumstances, be persuaded to have a mission in your parish till you know your people well. I once came to a parish and found myself practically committed to a parochial mission within six months. I lacked courage to withdraw, and the mission was held. But it was a complete failure and, except of course in individual cases, did harm and not good. The second caution is, Never have a mission because you feel things are not going well in the parish, and hope that a mission may improve matters. A mission is not, and should not be, a substitute for earnest pastoral work, or a cure for lack of success in such work. Rather it ought to be merely a means of garnering to the full the fruits of such work, and a parish which is going to have a mission should be at its healthiest and best. I sometimes wonder whether the comparative disrepute into which parochial missions have fallen in some quarters may not be due to failure to remember this fact. The third caution is, Never suppose that any gifts or graces on the part of the missioner can supply the lack of careful preparation by the parish clergy beforehand. Earnest preparation, and above all, earnest preparatory prayer by the clergy and all the faithful, and diligent visitation of the parish for weeks and months beforehand, are of more importance than the gifts or personality of the missioner. Without these a gifted missioner may be able, most unhappily, to prevent the mission from being seen to be a failure. He cannot prevent its being one.

(xv) Finally, I would say to every parish priest, Do not be always trying something fresh; do not be in a hurry. Many things, many methods of work, are described in this and the earlier chapters, and many others, possibly far more valuable, will suggest themselves to any keen and earnest parish priest. But it would be fatal to try them all at once, or even in quick succession. We are sent to lead, not to drive, our flocks, and the words of Jacob to Esau when he said, 'If men should overdrive them one day, all the flock will die,' contain a valuable lesson. And above all, when you want to start anything fresh, and to make a forward movement, wait for a suitable opportunity. Much depends, in parish work as in other things, on the ability to

> 'Know the seasons, when to take occasion by the hand.'

Let what you do be prompted, that is to say, not

by the mere desire to attempt something new, but by a desire to meet an obvious need. And when you decide on any new effort, do not spring it suddenly on the parish, but talk about it, explain its nature and object, solicit the help, sympathy, and prayers of the congregation, and make them feel interested in its success. And if what you are starting is not a mere passing effort, such as the Lent Convention or the Rogation-tide procession, but something which is meant to become a permanent part of the organisation of the parish, such as the monthly classes in preparation for Holy Communion, or the weekly dinner-hour service for workers in the neighbourhood, don't start it till you have weighed the cost and are sure you can keep it up. Nothing does more harm in a parish than the constant starting of new organisations which fall into neglect and decay almost as soon as they are born. And when you have started anything stick to it till it has become well established. Most things in a parish are a success while the novelty lasts. Then comes a danger period when numbers fall off rapidly. But if the man in charge sticks doggedly to his work numbers go up again, not perhaps to their first level, but to such a point as proves that the organisation was wanted. And when any venture has fallen from its highest to its lowest point, and then risen to a settled level somewhere between those two extremes, it may be regarded as fully established. Then, if well and carefully worked, it will grow steadily with a natural and healthy growth. But nothing is more hopeless than the attempt to revive something which has been allowed